SUZUKI VITARA

SUZUKI VITARA

THE ENTHUSIAST'S COMPANION

NIGEL FRYATT

MRP

MOTOR RACING PUBLICATIONS LTD
Unit 6, The Pilton Estate, 46 Pitlake, Croydon CR0 3RY, England

First published 1995

British Library Cataloguing in Publication Data
Fryatt, Nigel
 Suzuki Vitara:Enthusiast's Companion
 I. Title
 629.2222
 ISBN 0-947981-93-4

Photoset by JDB Typesetting, Croydon
Printed in Great Britain by
The Amadeus Press Ltd
Huddersfield, West Yorkshire

CONTENTS

Introduction

Today, Suzuki's multi-purpose Vitara holds an important position in the world of four-wheel drive vehicles. Yet its UK introduction back in 1988 caused quite a stir. Following in the successful path created by the Suzuki SJ range, the Vitara's chunky good looks were quite a significant surprise to the automotive establishment and it is fair to say that no other four-wheel drive vehicle on the market at the time came close to matching this new trend-setting Japanese design. Indeed, some commentators questioned whether the vehicle's looks were too radical. They asked whether the Vitara was supposed to be a road car for the fashion-conscious, and as such was therefore far too good-looking to be used off-road with the same enthusiasm as its SJ model predecessors.

Yet the Vitara is considerably more than just a vehicle with highly individual good looks. Strip off that smart body and you find a tough ladder-frame chassis and suspension set-up that confirms its intention to be more than just capable when taken off-road. And for anyone who has driven the Vitara to the limit on the rough stuff, you soon get to acknowledge that this is no pretty powder-puff of a machine: this is an off-roader of the highest order.

Suzuki Vitara: An Enthusiast's Companion's is aimed directly at those people who already own one of these multi-purpose vehicles and those who might be thinking of buying one. Angles covered include description of the vehicle's model range plus an easy-to-understand technical analysis, right through to a detailing of Suzuki's own Rhino Club and the unique socializing benefits that come from ownership.

Owners are taken through the aspects of Vitara servicing – something that is very important with this type of vehicle – and even if you never intend to do any of this work yourself, it is always worthwhile knowing exactly what is going on when you take your vehicle in for a service!

You may, however, be thinking about buying a secondhand Vitara, and perhaps this will be your first four-wheel drive vehicle; if so, just what should you look for? Helpful and understandable technical advice is designed to offer prospective purchasers peace of mind as well as practical advice.

Examination, too, is made of all the interesting accessories that are available to enable you to turn your Vitara into a highly personalized vehicle, as only true enthusiasts can do. Should you, for instance, fit a set of wide wheels to your Vitara? The options are assessed along with the possible disadvantages if you take things just a step too far.

One point all Vitara owners should consider is that first giant step off the tarmac and on to the rough stuff. For many, this may seem a daunting move and therefore some simple advice is offered to the novice Vitara off-road driver. One thing is certain though: the Vitara was designed to be taken off-

road and once you have tried it, driving will never be the same again.

Finally, I would like to acknowledge the help given by Suzuki GB's Marketing Director, Ian Catford, as well as Mike McNulty and Peter Smith from the company's technical and servicing departments. Some of the photographs included are from *Off Road & 4 Wheel Drive* magazine's archives, taken by experienced lensmen Norman Hodson and Tony Butler. Biggest thanks, however, has to go to the Vitara itself since this is one four-wheel drive vehicle that has never failed to produce the goods while at the same time proving highly entertaining. I can only hope that this *Enthusiast's Companion* has much the same qualities.

Nigel Fryatt

January 1995

Developing an image

The history of the Vitara

You cannot begin a book dedicated to the Suzuki Vitara without first looking back at the SJ range that preceded it. These small, jeep-like machines have had a significant impact on the UK four-wheel drive market as a whole, quite apart from the superb job of paving the way for the Vitara. The SJ offered affordable off-road fun, but it also started its very own fashion trend. It became a statement for the image-conscious Eighties, and the spartan, utilitarian design quickly became embellished with fancy paintwork and a whole variety of accessories to appeal to far more people than those who like to take their cars and get stuck in the mud. It is highly significant to record that 14 years after its UK introduction, the SJ soft-top remains in the Suzuki

The introduction of the Suzuki Vitara in 1988 caused a tremendous stir in the four-wheel drive market. The new bodyshape was very different and quite unexpected at the time.

No book on the Vitara would be complete without the SJ. The small utilitarian jeep brought a great many new people into the world of four-wheel drive. The SJ Santana remained in production after the launch of the Vitara.

price list, confirming the company's initial promise that the Vitara was not launched to replace the SJ, but merely to complement the four-wheel drive range. Such a period is impressive by modern automotive life spans.

Yet if the SJ enabled Suzuki to step to the forefront of automotive off-road fashion, the Vitara took full advantage of that reputation to take an important giant stride ahead. The Vitara provided the public with something that simply was not available anywhere else.

This was obvious the first time you saw the vehicle. Gone was the military look of the SJ jeep, and at 143 inches the Vitara was eight inches longer and some 20 per cent heavier than the SJ. It was a stylish, modern, four-wheel drive vehicle that Suzuki proudly claimed was "styled to new adventures for new lifestyles". The Japanese design team had produced a winning look that set its own standards and opened up new areas for sales.

Suzuki Japan decided that the British importer, Suzuki GB Cars, then a division of the Heron corporation, should be responsible for the European launch of the new Vitara in October 1988. This impressive operation took place in Edinburgh, Scotland with the vehicle's first public appearance being made at the British International Motor Show that same year. The importance of the launch was confirmed by the attendance in Scotland of Suzuki's President, Mr Osamu Suzuki. For the management of Suzuki GB, therefore, the whole operation had to be conducted on a grand scale. In the course of two or three days they had some 200-plus journalists from all over Europe test-drive a total of 70 new Vitaras. The designated route incorporated comprehensive on-road mileage, including motorway driving, passing through some official Scottish green lanes and then over a reasonably tough off-road course in a *bing* – formally an open cast mine. It is worthwhile commenting here that some manufacturer's four-wheel drive new vehicle launches concentrate 100 per cent on a tarmac test route and actively seem to deter you from taking the vehicle off-road. This has never been the case

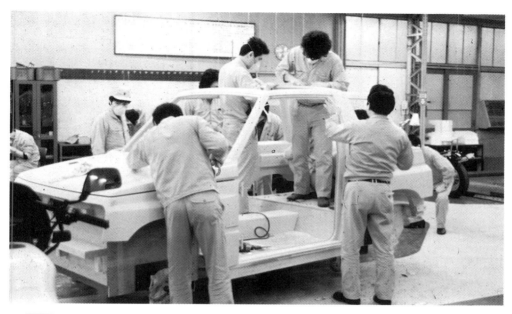

The design of the Vitara was achieved by the Japanese themselves. Here the team are working on a wooden mock-up, highlighting those now very familiar wheelarch extensions.

The five-door Vitara appeals to a different market: very much the family vehicle.

with Suzuki GB, the management taking the view that since the vehicle is very capable off-road, they expect journalists to test it there. It's a refreshing and commendable outlook.

Indeed, it is this kind of attitude that achieves the desired results. The ensuing feedback from the Scottish launch was extremely positive, especially since there were many European journalists who had never driven off-road before. Their first impressions of the Vitara were that it looked an attractive, rounded road car and that it drove very well on-road – far better, thanks to the completely new suspension, than the SJ range. The green lane section of the test-drive was relatively soft and easy, but it was the full off-road course constructed in the *bing* that caused the most surprises. Little of the SJ's acknowledged reputation in the rough stuff had been lost with the Vitara; in many ways it had been improved. If you look at the construction of the SJ, the design is 60 per cent off-road, 40 per cent on-road. With the Vitara these figures are reversed, the change round being the direct intention of the Japanese manufacturer.

The name Vitara is one of those artificially constructed names to imply lifestyle, youth and vitality, and was produced by a trademark name company in the UK. In Japan, new names are often decided on the basis of how they look graphically – which is why you occasionally get some odd ones, like the moped called Carrot! In the Japanese home market, Suzuki's new four-wheel drive was christened Escudo and this was to represent "The Evolution of Design Excellence".

Now, while the glossy and dramatic marketing formula should rightly be taken with a pinch of salt, there are certainly aspects of the Japanese

The soft-top Vitara has a fun image for those both young and young at heart who enjoy wind-in-the-hair motoring.

In its home country, the Vitara is marketed as the Escudo, designed to represent the evolution of design excellence.

promotion that help elucidate Suzuki's underlying philosophy for the vehicle. This is one four-wheel drive that is very much at home in the city, yet will meet any off-road challenge new owners are likely to throw at it. As the Japanese brochure underlines, the vehicle is for owners who "often get the urge to cast off formalities and head into the hills".

In the hills and highlands of that 1988 Scottish launch, the European market was offered two versions of the Vitara: the three door 'metal top', and then

Both in right and left-hand-drive variants, the Vitara's interior had come a long way from the original SJ concept. This was a small, relatively inexpensive four-wheel drive vehicle with all the comforts expected of a mainstream 'car'.

For many, it's the three-door body shape that best emphasizes the Vitara's good looks.

Short and relatively stubby at the rear, the three-door Vitara demonstrates a remarkable versatility with its folding rear seats that can increase the load area considerably.

early the following year, the soft-top. There were two levels of trim, JX or JLX. The top of the range model was the JLX Power Package which had the additions of power steering, power-operated window lifts, power door locks (central locking) and power adjustable door mirrors.

The highly individual body shape of the three-door version with its chunky appeal was enhanced by the pronounced wide wheelarches. The interior design was another important step away from the previous SJ, since it was well up to the standard expected of a 'normal' road car. There was no longer the excuse that since this was a jeep, the interior could be rather spartan and, let's face it, uncomfortable. The Vitara came with cloth seats, fully trimmed with hard-wearing carpets and smart, contoured facia and instrument panel.

Underneath this new body, the Vitara owed nothing to the SJ, the mechanicals matching the step forward achieved by the vehicle's looks and appointment. The Vitara's technical description is detailed in the following chapter, suffice to say here that initial models had the then all-new 1,590cc four-cylinder engine, five-speed gearbox with part-time four-wheel drive system and integrated two-speed transfer 'box. Gone were the ancient leaf springs used on the SJs, to be replaced with an up-to-date independent front, trailing link rear suspension with coil springs over shock absorbers. This development alone brought the Vitara the on-road ride and handling characteristics that would make it appeal to a far greater market than those who seem to enjoy the pitching 'bucking bronco' characteristics of leaf-sprung off-roaders.

Remarkably quickly after the initial launch, Suzuki kept Vitara interest high when the automatic version was shown at the 1989 Motorfair at Earls Court. It was the first small-engined, four-wheel drive vehicle to be made available with a three-speed automatic transmission and in many respects was a surprising move for the company to make.

Rather more expected was the introduction of fuel injected, catalyzed versions of the 1.6-litre engine in July 1991. Nowadays, due to emission legislation, carburettors tend to be viewed as somewhat 'classic' automotive technology, quite apart from the fact that injected engines are smoother, more responsive and in this case more powerful. The power output increase was modest, up from 74 to 80bhp, torque now at 94lb.ft at 3,000rpm, but it did extend the vehicle's towing limit from 1,100kg to 1,450kg.

Obviously the most significant development of the Vitara's model range came with the July 1991 announcement of the five-door Estate. The longer wheelbase took the Vitara's chunky, flared wheelarch design very well and once again opened the vehicle to a new customer base, which recent Suzuki GB plc market research has confirmed. Those buying three-door Vitaras are equally spread 50/50, male/female, although primary users of the three-door models are 70 per cent female, indicating that in many cases the three-door Vitara is often the second car in a household. For the five-door, however, 80 per cent of buyers are male and when you look at the primary driver male/female ratio, this increases to 90 per cent male. The five-door Vitara is, therefore, far more likely to be a family's number one vehicle.

Yet the five-door Estate's introduction brought more than just increased legroom and luggage area: it also had a new development of the 1.6-litre engine. A completely redesigned cylinder head now had four valves per cylinder with multi-point fuel injection and a three-way catalytic converter. This 16v unit offered a 15bhp power increase over the 8v unit, pushing it up to 95bhp at 5,600rpm. The engine's torque characteristics improved only by four per cent to 97.7lb.ft. Of course, the increase was necessary for the increased weight of the five-door and the larger loads that it had been designed to carry.

A five-speed manual version is available, but most of the interest has been with the automatic since this saw the introduction of the completely new four-speed automatic transmission, with its **Power** and **Normal** modes (see second and third chapters) to suit driving style and conditions.

In Japan, the five-door Vitara is called the Nomade which is a far more evocative name than 'Estate'. However, the UK marketing philosophy was more obviously directed towards winning over buyers who might otherwise consider buying a normal 'estate' car.

Besides Japan and Europe, the Vitara is building a reputation in America. General Motors' shareholding in the Japanese company has led to the vehicle being marketed through the Geo dealer network (this also markets Suzuki saloons and the five-door Estate model as the Suzuki Sidekick). The American Vitara is known as the Geo Tracker and has some interesting technical differences from the UK models, not the least of which is the fact that one model is available as two-wheel drive only! This means there are two convertible versions of the Tracker in two and four-wheel drive, together with a hard-topped, four-wheel drive version. All US Trackers have rear-wheel anti-lock brakes.

The American four-wheel drive market differs greatly from that in either Japan or Europe. It's fair to comment that they like them big in the States, but it seems that the Tracker is beginning to win over friends as a couple of the convertibles have been seen on US detective TV series, although quite whether they are two or four-wheel drive is not so clear!

Back in the UK during the summer of 1993, there were two new models introduced, in some respects aimed at opposite ends of the market. The two-seater Vitara Sport came in as the cheapest model in the range, of which there are actually two versions, one with and one without windows in the detachable hood – the latter therefore being classed as a commercial on

In the United States, the Vitara is sold under General Motors Geo range, titled the Tracker. Interestingly, there is even a two-wheel drive version in the Geo Tracker US brochure!

The Vitara X-EC was a limited edition version with a higher level of equipment than its standard five-door brother.

which VAT can be reclaimed. The Sport, still in carburettor form, remains the cheapest Vitara available.

At the other end of the market, 1993 saw the introduction of the X-EC which was first seen as a concept vehicle at the 1992 British Motor Show at Birmingham. Under the bright lights at the NEC, the concept Vitara had exotic paintwork, leather interior and super sexy alloy wheels. Unfortunately, the resultant production X-EC has to be seen as something of a disappointment. Gone is the leather and alloy wheels, although it does have Deep Blue Pearl metallic paint, automatic **free-wheeling** front **hubs** and limited slip differential as standard.

Special editions have been an important way for Suzuki GB plc to keep the Vitara in the news. The 1994 Vitara Verdi and Vitara Rossini are two classy-looking, cheekily-named models that are painted Polynesian Green and Montego Bay Magenta – lime green and pinky red to you and me – both with white soft-tops.

The Verdi and Rossini look good, but don't have anything extra to offer the four-wheel drive enthusiast. As if to underline this, late 1994 has seen the Vitara come up against some impressive competitors, notably Toyota's RAV4 which is aimed squarely at Suzuki customers. If the RAV4 has an appealing shape, a quick look at its technical specification – monocoque body construction, permanent four-wheel drive yet with no transfer 'box, so no low ratio gears – means that it is no match for the Vitara when taken off-road. Suzuki Japan can obviously see the danger from these new competitors,

Special editions have been a trademark of Suzuki GB's overall marketing philosophy. The Rossini shown here has a special metallic paintwork, sexy alloy wheels and a smart interior. When launched in 1994, Suzuki claimed that the Rossini had 'elegance and distinction in perfect harmony'. Well, you know what these marketing people are like...

These Suzuki design studies, sent to the author from Japan just for inclusion in this book, show that the Japanese studio still has a great deal of enthusiasm for the Vitara. Of course, you may not see these in production.

however, and it is certain that the Vitara is set to develop further, as the concept X/90 vehicle clearly shows.

As 1995 begins and the Vitara enters its seventh year, management changes have seen Suzuki GB Cars as no longer part of the Heron corporation, now being registered as Suzuki GB plc. This has had little effect on Vitara owners, although the changeover did lead to the cancellation of the 1994 Rhino Rally.

The Vitara ended 1994 as the the third highest selling 4x4 in the UK, taking an impressive 10 per cent of the market. In total, worldwide, there have been some 710,000 Vitaras exported, but there is little chance of the company

Making the rounds of the major motor shows in 1994 was the Suzuki X/90 concept vehicle. Still recognizable as a Vitara, could this be the future thinking of the company?

becoming complacent. Indeed, as this *Enthusiast's Companion* was being completed, two new developments were announced which make the future look particularly bright.

The first announcement was to be expected and that sees the 16-valve version of the engine fitted in the three-door Vitara JLX SE. This makes a sensible natural progression and is a trend that would be expected to continue across the range with the eight-valve unit being eventually phased

Present at the 1994 British Motor Show was this concept vehicle from Suzuki GB, the Extreme. The 'bolt-on' wheelarch and bumper effect was not to everyone's liking it has to be said; it almost makes a Vitara look more like a Santana. Suzuki GB have gone into limited production in the UK, built to special order.

The 16-valve version of the trusty 1,600cc power unit is available in the top of the range three-door JLX SE.

out completely.

The rather more exciting development for the Vitara was the announcement just before Christmas 1994 of a brand-new engine for the five-door Estate: the Suzuki-designed, 2-litre V6, which will take the Vitara into yet another market sector; at the time of its launch there was no other small, V6-engined 4x4 available on the UK market.

The latest Vitara V6 has a redesigned front grille, bumpers and additional chrome work.

The V6 Vitara has smart 16in wheels and is fitted with 215/65 section tyres.

Suzuki describe the facia in the Vitara V6 as having 'executive car style instrumentation'.

The 1,998cc 24-valve, V6 power unit has twin overhead camshafts and multi-point fuel injection delivering 134bhp at a relatively high 6,500rpm and 127lb.ft of torque at 4,000rpm. This compact V6 is a neat design and is available with either the five-speed manual gearbox or the four-speed automatic with its **Power** and **Economy** modes. It is fitted with the familiar part-time, two-speed, transfer box. The V6 model also has automatic **free-wheeling** front **hubs** – discussed in the next section – so there is no getting your hands dirty switching them as there is with the manual variety!

The economy claims are very impressive since at a constant 56mph (with the manual gearbox) and the 15.4-gallon fuel tank, a range in excess of 500 miles could be possible. It's likely, however, that Vitara owners concerned about increased miles per gallon will wait for the diesel-engined version.

Although there aren't any major differences to the V6 Vitara Estate's exterior appearance, you can easily spot this top of the range model. Its wheelbase is the same as other five-door models, thanks to the chassis and suspension, but the V6 is 95mm longer and 65mm wider – apparent from the contoured wheelarch extensions and larger front and rear bumpers. Under those wider

Designed by Suzuki, the V6 engine has 24 valves, twin overhead camshafts and multi-point fuel injection. It produces 134bhp at 6,500rpm and 127lb.ft of torque at 4,000rpm.

arches are 16in wheels fitted with 215/65 section tyres.

Inside, the V6 has the latest instrument panel and switchgear and different seat cloth from any other Vitara model. As would be expected, specification is high, comprising airbags, power steering, electric windows and mirrors,

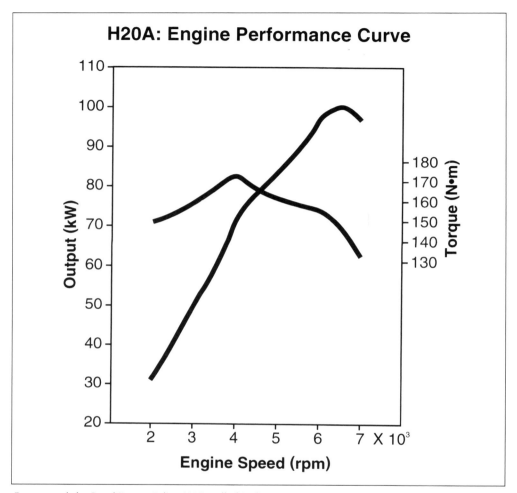

Power graph for Suzuki's new 2-litre V6 installed in the Vitara estate.

central locking fitted as standard and optional extras including ABS braking, alloy wheels and sunroof.

Unfortunately, the V6 was launched at the very time of this *Enthusiast's Companion* going to print which means that we were unable to drive it before the presses rolled. However, it is fairly certain that the increased power will improve the on-road performance, while the engine's torque will be excellent for those owners who take the machine into the rough stuff off-road. The slightly wider front and rear track should more than cope with the increased performance making the V6 an excellent handling machine.

Personally, I would like to see the V6 engine fitted to the three-door Vitara . . . and who knows? One thing that is certain though: the Suzuki Vitara's future is assured.

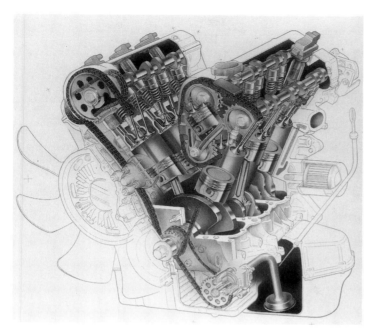

Cutaway of the all-new 2-litre V6 DOHC power-unit.

The V6 interior has uprated seat cloth to give that quality look.

Getting technical

Understanding the Vitara

The Suzuki Vitara is not a highly complex machine. Yet this statement in no way detracts from the vehicle's qualities – in fact, it enhances them. All the best designs are relatively simple, and with a multi-purpose four-wheel drive machine like the Vitara, you do not want a complicated specification that might by its very nature prove to be temperamental or even unreliable.

Although a modern design, the Suzuki Vitara follows some very traditional four-wheel drive principles. For a start, it has a separate, three-section ladder-frame chassis with a central bracing bar to prevent excessive twisting. This

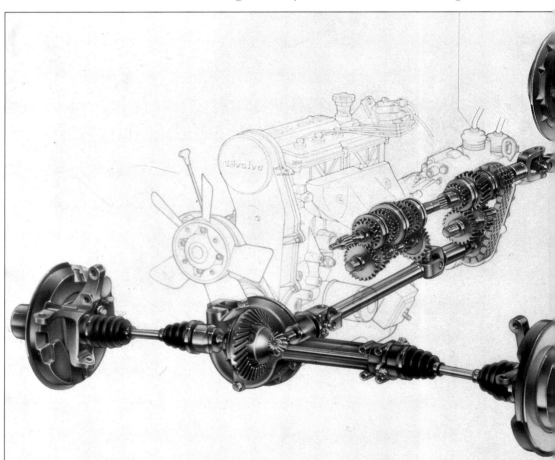

provides a sturdy backbone to the vehicle on to which the suspension and driveline are connected. The relatively lightweight body sits on top of the whole lot, rubber-mounted to the chassis where necessary to reduce vibration and harshness. It is therefore separate from the chassis and suspension, and remains relatively unstressed during even the most serious off-roading. This should aid the longevity of the vehicle and prevent any annoying creaks and squeaks developing in the bodyshell caused by excessive flexing, for even the most enthusiastic off-roading owner.

On a further practical point, much of the lower body panels and chassis have been galvanized against corrosion, which is useful both for those poor winters or fun afternoons when you are wading your Vitara off-road and in the water!

If the ladder-type chassis shows Suzuki's engineers to be appreciative of good off-road traditions, the rear suspension also indicates that they are not

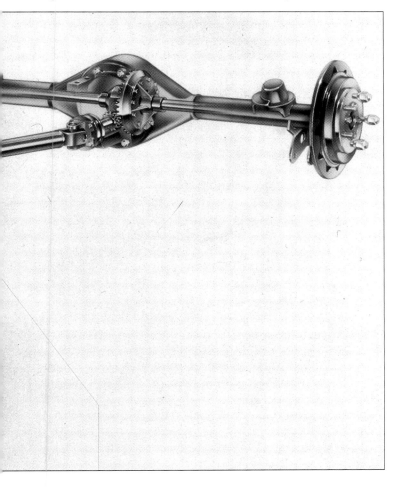

The Suzuki's four-wheel drive system is relatively simple and straightforward – and all the better for it. In two-wheel drive the engine is turning the rear wheels; when four-wheel drive is selected, drive is also transferred to the front.

Under the attractive bodystyle, the Vitara exhibits its strong, sturdy, ladder-frame chassis. In this picture, the trolley jack is actually raising the front of the vehicle on one arm of that chassis. At the rear, the chassis frame can be seen curving up and over the rear axle.

afraid to use principles from some of the best off-road machines. With the Vitara's live rear axle located by coil springs and trailing lower links and a short centre A-frame (which picks up on the differential), you could be forgiven for thinking this design has been inspired by products from the Land Rover catalogue – and if it's good enough for them....

At the front the Vitara has fully independent suspension, with those familiar coil springs and MacPherson struts. These allow for particularly good wheel articulation – vital for any decent off-roader. Also important are good **Approach** and **Departure** angles. These are the angles between the ground and the front and rear overhang of the bodywork: if there is too much bodywork and bumper ahead of the front wheels you will have difficulty, when off-road, riding up a slope or over an object. In this respect, good off-road machines are said to 'have a wheel at each corner' and this is certainly true of the Vitara with its front and rear Approach and Departure angles of 40deg and 41deg respectively.

There is limited **underbody ground clearance** of only eight inches and the vehicle's **ramp break-over angle** is only 25deg – which is not particularly impressive, but this is compensated by the aforementioned wheel and axle

The Vitara's lower body and underside is fully galvanized against corrosion, which helps during both poor winters and those times when you take the Vitara into the wet and muddy stuff!

The Vitara's suspension set-up is fully independent at the front with MacPherson struts and coil springs, which allows for excellent wheel articulation. The rear axle is located by coil springs and trailing lower links.

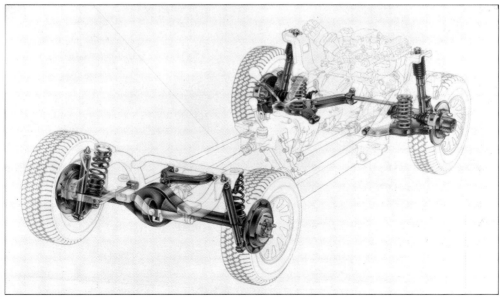

At the Vitara's launch, much emphasis was made of the qualities underneath the new eye-catching bodywork.

articulation. Indeed, the whole suspension design offers a good compromise in the ride/handling, on and off-road argument. It is certainly a significant step forward over the previous SJ range.

The Vitara's solid chassis arrangement has allowed for a relatively light body, which in turn has meant that Suzuki could use a relatively small capacity engine. The Suzuki G16A, four-cylinder, all-alloy engine of 1,590cc, is a relatively long stroke, single overhead camshaft unit which had been designed specifically for the Vitara. By using alloy materials and a hollow crankshaft and camshaft, the unit is light and has reasonable torque characteristics when you take into account the actual capacity of the engine. However, the slight disadvantage of these lightened components is that the engine does sound a little harsh at high revs.

The first UK versions were fitted with twin-choke carburettors and offered a power output of 74bhp (55kW) at 5,250rpm and torque of 90lb.ft (122.5Nm) at only 3,100rpm. The engine has since enjoyed some notable developments throughout the Vitara's short history: electronic fuel injection came first, followed by a reworking of the cylinder head for the 16v version that arrived with the five-door Estate. Still a single overhead camshaft unit, the 16v version produces a healthy 95bhp at a slightly higher 5,600rpm and 97.7lb.ft of torque at 4,000rpm (again at a higher point in the rev range, a standard characteristic of a multi-valve power unit). As would be expected, the engine has a three-way catalytic converter with the standard 'closed loop' oxygen sensor monitored by the engine's computer to regulate carefully the fuelling

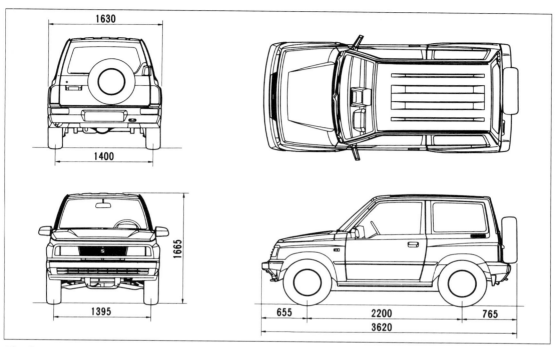

The dimensions, in millimetres, of the three-door Vitara showing the 'wheel at each corner' principle to good effect.

of the injection system under differing conditions.

Fuel economy for the 16v engine in the five-door Vitara fitted with manual transmission, is 36.7mpg at a constant 56mph. Perhaps more impressive is the fact that when fitted with the four-speed automatic transmission, the Vitara Estate's consumption only drops to 35.8mpg.

The Vitara's drivetrain follows Suzuki's belief in part-time four-wheel drive, keeping the Vitara as a rear-wheel drive on-road car, with the four-wheel drive system only to be engaged off-road or when the road surface is extremely slippery. The 'normal' gearbox has an integrated two-speed transfer 'box to allow drive to be transmitted to the front wheels when four-wheel drive is selected. The design is described by Suzuki as a 'centre through format' in that it directly links the transmission with the transfer 'box thus making unnecessary an additional driveshaft. The transfer gears transmit power via a chaindrive to the forward propshaft and thus the front wheels. It's a neat and simple design, allowing for very slick and precise gear-changing with very little transmission whine – something that can be a problem with other four-wheel drive vehicles.

The four-speed automatic transmission that became an option with the launch of the five-door Vitara Estate, offers a particularly smooth gear change since the actual shifting is controlled electronically and 4th gear is a

*The first models were
introduced with the G16A
four-cylinder, all-alloy
engine of 1,590cc. This
single overhead camshaft
unit was designed and built
specifically for the Vitara.*

selectable overdrive. On 3rd and 4th gears the gearbox has a lock-up torque converter which engages at a set cruising speed, to transmit the power directly from the engine. This makes the unit both quieter and more efficient, hence the impressive fuel consumption figures.

The four-speed automatic Vitara's fuel economy is further helped by the **Power** and **Normal** option on the transmission. These simply dictate when the gearbox will change up a gear: in Power it holds on to a low ratio longer and thus you will get better acceleration. In Normal mode, the gearchanges are optimized for efficiency, changing up earlier in the rev range which is therefore quieter and more fuel efficient.

Four-wheel drive is simply engaged by moving the 'second' gear lever into 4H (high ratio) or 4L (low ratio). It's a simple procedure but there are just a couple of points that an inexperienced four-wheel driver should appreciate here.

Free-wheeling hubs are an option for the Vitara and their principle is simple, but sometimes misunderstood. When the vehicle is in two-wheel drive, the engine is turning the rear wheels. By the very motion of the vehicle,

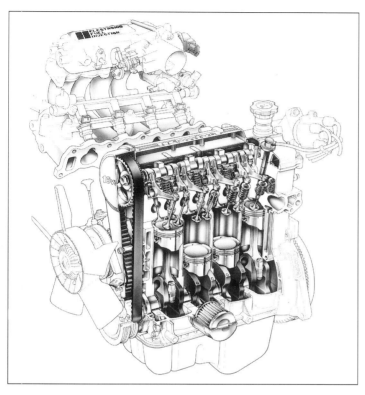

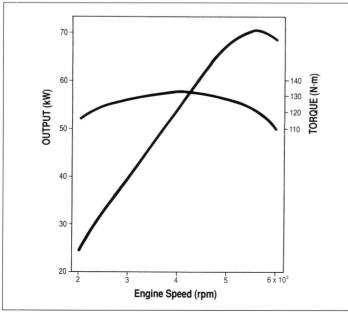

The G16B Vitara power unit includes the advantages of 16 valves and fuel injection. As the performance graph shows quite clearly, the fuel injected unit has a fairly smooth torque curve – essential for a good off-road machine.

Under the bonnet the latest version of the 16v power unit fits snugly into the Vitara's engine bay.

the front wheels will still be turning the front driveshafts, front differential and forward propshaft. Obviously more effort is needed to do this and there will be some noise associated with these various mechanical parts rotating. Free-wheel hubs effectively disconnect the front wheels from all this, so that they rotate freely while the associated bits and pieces of the front drivetrain are no longer turning. Over a period of time, an owner with free-wheeling hubs will probably notice slightly better fuel economy and less noise from the transmission.

When going off-road, if your vehicle is fitted with free-wheeling front hubs you will need to ensure they are engaged, otherwise you will remain in two-wheel drive even when you think you have selected 4H. If they are manual hubs, this will involve twisting the centre to the LOCK position – obvious really! If you have automatic hubs, you will not need to worry about engaging them, but it is important to remember when you have finished off-roading and selected two-wheel drive, that you have to reverse the vehicle a few yards to disengage the hubs. With some practice you may be able to hear them actually disengage as you reverse.

The Suzuki's four-wheel drive system is only to be used off-road or when there is a serious amount of slippage between tyre and the road surface – even on wet roads it will probably not slip sufficiently to make this necessary.

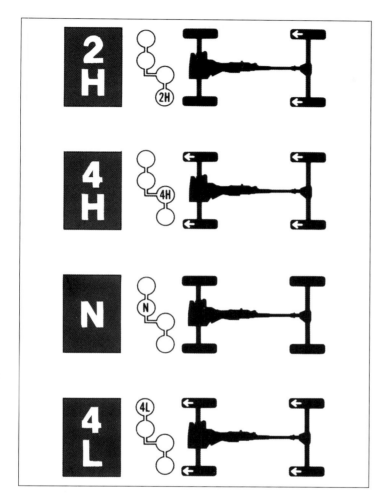

This simple schematic diagram best illustrates exactly which wheels are being driven when the Suzuki Vitara's gear-lever is in a particular position. 2H is for normal road use, through to 4L which is needed for when the going gets tough off-road.

If there is not enough slippage you could find yourself grinding to a complete stop with **transmission wind-up**. This occurs when the equal amount of drive is being transferred to both front and rear wheels but since there is no centre differential in a Vitara to allow for any differences in wheel rotations front and rear when cornering, the whole drivetrain will more or less tie itself up in a knot! Transmission wind-up has caught out many a new Vitara driver. The good news is that if it winds itself up too much, it will just stall the engine and should not break halfshafts. Of course, if you keep doing it....

Suzuki are well aware that new owners need to understand fully about their vehicle's four-wheel drive system and as a consequence are training their dealers to try to ensure problems like transmission wind-up do not happen.

As will be covered later, Suzuki are strongly against oversized wheels and tyres being fitted to the Vitara. This is obviously a personal decision for the

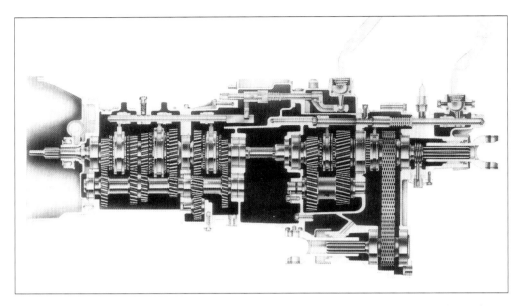

This cutaway drawing of the Vitara's transmission clearly shows the centre-through format of the gearbox. The lever on the left is the standard gear shift, whereas the smaller one on the right operates the transfer box for all four-wheel drive applications.

owner but if individual preference is forgotten for a moment, it is worth considering the technical reasons as to why this is so. "The physics of the thing are all wrong," explains Michael McNulty, Technical Training Manager for Suzuki GB plc. "The problem you have with the Vitara is that there is a very narrow clearance between the standard inner tyre wall and the suspension. Therefore, the only way to get wide wheels to fit is to extend the off-set, through the centre line of the hub if you like. This means that to put a 10inch-wide wheel on, you are off-setting anything up to 35mm, which is a considerable amount.

"By doing this you are increasing the loading on the steering and the drivetrain simply because of the extra friction of the rolling resistance of the tyre. A 255-section tyre has got a much greater coefficient of drag than a 195. Also, because of the off-set you are putting external loadings on to the wheel bearings that are not present with the standard zero off-set wheel.

"In simple terms, the Vitara's suspension has not been designed to take these loadings."

Obviously, it comes down to a matter of choice and common sense on behalf of the owner. To steer a middle ground here, a seven or maybe eight-inch wheel really ought to be the maximum anyone should consider, and if you do intend to off-road your Vitara, great big fat wheels are not going to be much of a help anyway.

So those are the technicalities behind the Vitara. Certainly it is not too

The Vitara's four-speed automatic gearbox is something of a major achievement. This kind of technical option is usually associated with much bigger – and far more expensive – four-wheel drive models.

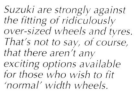

Suzuki are strongly against the fitting of ridiculously over-sized wheels and tyres. That's not to say, of course, that there aren't any exciting options available for those who wish to fit 'normal' width wheels.

complex, but it does succeed in meeting the parameters for which it was designed. A good multi-purpose, four-wheel drive really needs a strong separate chassis, good wheel and axle articulation and a willing engine – and those three areas are exactly what you find when you look underneath a Vitara's smart exterior.

Specifications

SUZUKI VITARA SPORT three-door

ENGINE
Type	G16A (8-valve SOHC) Four-cylinder
Bore	75.0mm
Stroke	90.0mm
Capacity	1,590cc
Compression ratio	8.9:1
Maximum power	74bhp @ 5,200rpm
Maximum torque	90lb.ft @ 3,100rpm

TRANSMISSION
Manual	Five-speed with part-time transfer box

SUSPENSION
Front	Independent, MacPherson strut, coil spring and wishbones
Rear	Live rear axle, coil springs, trailing arm

WHEELS
Tyres (as Original Equipment)	195R15 94Q P205/75R 15 195SR 15 195/80R 15 94Q
Pressures (normal road driving)	23psi (front and rear)

DIMENSIONS
Wheelbase	2,200mm
Length	3,620mm
Width	1,630mm
Height	1,665mm
Track (front)	1,395mm
(rear)	1,400mm
Ground clearance	200mm
Gross vehicle weight	1,450kg
Kerb weight (manual)	1,020kg
(automatic)	1,125kg
Towing weight (braked)	450kg
(unbraked)	450kg
Fuel tank	42 litre

SUZUKI VITARA JLX SE five-door

ENGINE
Type	G16B (16-valve SOHC) Four-cylinder
Bore	75.0mm
Stroke	90.0mm
Capacity	1,590cc
Compression ratio	9.5:1
Maximum power	94.6bhp @ 5,600rpm
Maximum torque	97.7lb.ft @ 4,000rpm

TRANSMISSION
Manual	Five-speed with part-time transfer box
Automatic	Four-speed with part-time transfer box, lock-up torque convertor, switchable overdrive

SUSPENSION
Front	Independent, Mac-Pherson strut, coil spring and wishbones
Rear	Live rear axle, coil springs, trailing arm

WHEELS
Tyres (as Original Equipment)	195R15 94Q P205/75R 15 195SR 15 195/80R 15 94Q
Pressures (normal road driving)	23psi (front and rear)

DIMENSIONS
Wheelbase	2,480mm
Length	4,030mm
Width	1,635mm
Height	1,700mm
Track (front)	1,395mm
(rear)	1,400mm
Ground clearance	200mm
Gross vehicle weight	1,650kg
Kerb weight (manual)	1,195kg
(automatic)	1,215kg
Towing weight (braked)	680kg
(unbraked)	450kg
Fuel tank	55 litre

Double roadtest:

Suzuki Vitara Sport:
Lean, lively and a lot of fun

Over the past decade there have been a number of trends within the world of four-wheel drive vehicles. One particular direction has been to move the vehicles ridiculously upmarket, taking them to the point where the original 'off-road' premise has all but disappeared. When you move into the areas of leather seats, air-conditioning, multi-speaker stereo CD systems and other assorted bells and whistles, you have to question whether people actually know how to *enjoy* these vehicles

Perhaps ironically, while some have been moving their four-wheel drive range into regions where the vehicle's price could probably buy a small three-bedroomed semi in some parts of the country, Suzuki have kept their principles well intact and gone in the opposite direction. It is obvious that they have looked hard at the market and said, "Let's offer a vehicle that is built primarily for fun and let's make it affordable".

The Suzuki Vitara Sport is just such a vehicle, but its origins go back to the SJ range, in particular the Santana models, since the Vitara Sport comes into the UK from the Suzuki-Santana operation in Spain.

Now, as has been said in the first chapter, the Vitara is a much better vehicle than the SJ. It is a natural development, has a superior technical specification and is far more modern than the trusty 'old' SJ models. This is good news, since the original SJ410 Santana Sport came in for some valid criticism when it was introduced into the UK. There were questions about build quality which, when matched with the dated leaf spring suspension set-up, did a great deal to colour the initial reasoning behind the SJ Sport – that of producing a cheap, open-topped, fun vehicle.

With the Vitara Sport, there are no such worries. The build quality and presentation of the vehicle are well up to the very highest Japanese standards and that is important for both the new buyer and those who might be considering the vehicle as a secondhand purchase.

Keeping the price low is not done just as a philanthropic gesture on the part of the manufacturer. It is an important marketing tool, to place the car in an area where many more people can consider purchase. Of course, the economic methods making this move possible include stripping the base Sport model of all but the essentials.

Under the skin exists the now-familiar technical specification. In carburettor form, the 1,600cc four-cylinder is still offering those 74 enthusiastic horses

The Suzuki Vitara Sport comes complete with the fresh, youthful sporting image of a go-anywhere, have-fun machine. But of course, it's more than just image since the vehicle's physical characteristics make it ideal for all forms of sport.

The model tested here had the 74bhp version of the 1,600cc engine – enough perhaps, but a little more in the power department wouldn't go amiss.

In order to keep the price down, the Sport's interior is rather spartan, but it's comfortable nevertheless.

and it has the independent front, live axle rear suspension and chassis set-up. On top of that, Suzuki have provided a body without a roof, because as we all now know, giving a vehicle the 'Sport' synonym means fresh air, wind in the face and the occasional need for a pair of shorts and sunglasses.

Topless means the need for a hood and for the Vitara Sport this comes from the American Bestop company. Assorted Velcro, press studs, clips, hoops and heavy-duty zips contain the whole lot in place for the most inclement of weather. But when the sun just peeps from behind the clouds there is an ingenious variety of options to enable the owner to take full advantage. You can, for instance, keep the rear three quarters in place and take away the

Open to please: the Sport's soft-top nature offers a variety of different body styles to suit all occasions – ideal for the vagaries of the British weather.

central roof area. This allows for all the right fresh air feeling, and can quickly be covered when the weather turns nasty. Alternatively the top can be left up and the rear removed, which allows for all the fun of an open, pick-up style, car with no need to worry the minute the first few drops of rain fall, or the fact that you have a beautifully coiffured passenger who is particularly concerned about the wind! To finish off the versatility, there are also removable back and side windows.

It is fair to say that for new owners, working out just how all this comes apart and – more importantly – how it all goes back together, can be rather complicated but with practice this is not a problem and after all, is only a function of the Vitara Sport package's ingenuity.

Inside, the most obvious difference is the fact that the standard Vitara Sport only has two seats. This does seem a touch mean, because if you do have a vehicle like this, you can almost guarantee that you'll be the sort of person who has a few friends...yet you can only take one out at a time. However, a rear bench and rear seat belts are available as optional extras, so maybe I am being a little harsh.

You do get a stereo radio cassette player included, which is sensibly one of the removable kind – an essential feature for any open-topped car. On the option list is the neat steel strong box that is securely bolted underneath the passenger seat – a good idea and something that all owners ought to consider.

Mechanically familiar, driving the Sport is much the same as other Vitara models except that it doesn't come with power steering. This is obviously done to contain costs, is not a problem when on the move on the road and arguably allows for better 'feel' and control when on the rough stuff. The lack of power steering is not going to be a problem for owners that keep to the standard 195R15 Dunlop Qualifier radial tyres, but you could need to build up your biceps if you want to fit those outrageous super-wide monster wheels and tyres! The standard Sport wheels are simple steel affairs, also used on other models, being reasonably smart and ideal for off-roading because they are easy to clean.

The Suzuki Vitara Sport's other cost-cutting areas, apart from the power steering, are lack of a passenger grab handle above the door, there's no clock and the courtesy light switch only works on the driver's door. None of these features is particularly important, but what is perhaps the most ironic part of the whole exercise is that dealers very rarely sell a *basic* vehicle.

The Vitara Sport is where you *start* if you want to customize your vehicle. In standard form, for instance, the basic wheel and tyre combination and the very subdued 'Sport' graphics are particularly tame. This is the model that cries out for more graphics, for bull bars, and while I am not a lover of 'Carlos Fandango-style' wheels and tyres, a set of sensibly-sized alloys would be a major improvement.

The Sport has an acceptable ride on the road, especially when you bear in

There's no place for passengers in the Vitara Sport! In standard form, the Sport comes as a strict two-seater. For those with additional friends or maybe young children, a rear bench seat is available.

Surely something of a must for all Sport owners is the neat lockable security box that can be fitted under the front seat. This allows the vehicle's radio and other valuables to be locked away with reasonable confidence.

mind the short wheelbase. Performance is as would be expected, but take the roof down, wind down the windows, get to feel the elements and you will think that the Sport is a far brisker performer than other Vitaras – plus the fact that the short wheelbase certainly offers a touch of extra flexibility over the five-door version when it comes to taking to the rough stuff, and sensibly there is still suitable roll-over protection should you have a problem. Indeed, the fact that the Vitara Sport is designed with the integral roll-over bar protection also means that the lack of a roof does not create a flimsy body. Scuttle shake from the Sport is commendably limited, which is a plus point for any open-topped vehicle.

You can also have this open version as a commercial vehicle, in which case the lack of rear seats allows for added carrying capacity, although you would certainly need to have some sort of bulkhead between the rear carrying area and the front seats. Without this, items in the rear have a great habit of rolling through to the front footwells which is annoying and potentially dangerous should your weekly shopping suddenly become tangled up with the driver's pedals.

The Sport version was a natural development of the Vitara range and it is commendable that Suzuki used the opportunity to keep the cost of the basic vehicle as low as possible. Of course, in so doing they created a fun vehicle that is attractive but just cries out for all those enhancing little extras for you to personalize the machine fully. But that's business, after all. The only thing that you cannot buy is the necessary good weather to enjoy the Sport to the full.

Suzuki JLX SE five-door: Practicality with poise

The Vitara's compact package has done much to establish its position in the market. However, for some people it is too small, especially those with families who need an extra pair of doors. That is where the introduction in late 1991 of the five-door Vitara was so important.

Before its arrival, however, it was hard to look at the shape of the three-door model and envisage the extent to which a long wheelbase version could be produced without it looking like a small Transit van with wide wheelarches. That said, the resultant appearance has to be seen as something of a triumph for the designers since it slots the vehicle into a very neat area for those who

The five-door Vitara in its element – enjoying the elements. This is a family favourite, but can still perform remarkably well when taken off-road.

need four doors and extra space but do not want, or cannot afford, some of the very much larger five-door four-wheel drives on the market.

Perhaps the most important point is that the five-door Vitara so obviously resembles its three-door stablemate. The wheelarch body extensions that are the Vitara trademark have been carried over to the five-door model with no loss of style; indeed, for some the five-door has a slightly better balance.

A longer wheelbase means a heavier vehicle so it was appropriate that the model was introduced with the uprated 16v version of the 1,600cc engine, bringing with it a bonus of 15 extra bhp (up to 95bhp) and 98lb.ft of torque. This copes admirably with the extra weight of the vehicle – and far more importantly, the potential extra weight that the vehicle can carry.

The characteristics of the engine remain the same: multi-valve injected small capacity Japanese engines all need to be worked hard to get the best from them. Of course, that is not a problem for the Vitara's power unit, but it can be something of a culture shock for drivers brought up on the Ford-like philosophy that most people don't want to rev their engines above 4,000rpm. Once you have kicked that into touch and do not think that driving the engine into the 5,000-plus rpm band means you are some kind of maniacal Mansell clone, you will appreciate the vehicle far more.

The other significant change with the five-door Vitara was the option of the four-speed automatic gearbox. This gives the driver the option of allowing the car to shift gear electronically, with the fourth gear acting as an economically-minded overdrive. The gearbox also has a lock-up torque converter mechanism which means that above a set cruising speed in third and fourth gears there is direct drive from the engine through the gearbox. This is more efficient, should save fuel and is certainly much quieter for the occupants. You are also given the **Power** or **Normal** transmission modes. As explained in the previous chapter, in **Normal** setting the gearbox will change up earlier than when in the **Power** setting which will hang on and keep the engine revs running higher. Again the choice is between economy or the desire for that little extra zip in the vehicle's acceleration. It is, nonetheless, fair to say that this is a very good automatic gearbox and something that many potential five-door Vitara owners should consider.

The interior has the quality feel of the cloth upholstery but as you would expect, there's far more space: this is a family machine. The five-door Vitara also has a suitably large luggage area behind the rear seats – something that some manufacturers conveniently forget. Of course, if there are only two occupants the headrests can be removed, the front seats adjusted and tilted to match the rear seating and a decent night's kip can be had.

Behind the wheel on the tarmac, the extra wheelbase naturally helps to give the five-door a better ride than its shorter brother. This eradicates the unpleasant pitching sensation that nearly all 4x4s suffer from to some degree, the shorter the wheelbase the worse it being.

The well-equipped interior of the five-door Vitara JLX SE. The cloth seats look smart and more importantly, are very comfortable. The model driven was fitted with the four-speed automatic transmission.

In two-wheel drive form Vitaras drive just the rear wheels. When loaded up and pressing on with enthusiasm I would have to agree with the slight criticism that these vehicles would benefit from having a permanent four-wheel drive set-up. This opinion is particularly confirmed when driving on damp, mildly slippery roads. Somehow, the visually chunky-looking free-wheeling front hubs look out of place on the five-door Vitara and I am sure they confuse some potentials buyers and even owners.

Off-road, the five-door performs as admirably as the shorter Vitara with the obvious exception that the longer wheelbase must be taken into account

This cutaway picture of the five-door Vitara gives a good indication of the vehicle's impressive load-carrying capacity, the drawing showing the side-impact bars in the doors of the Vitara estate.

when cresting small hills or crossing ridges. The machine has generous Approach and Departure angles so that owners can really 'have a go' with it. Once again the thanks must go to the ladder-frame chassis, the coil sprung suspension, a low centre of gravity and good axle articulation.

Galvanized panels and decent waterproofing also mean that the Vitara five-door can take a little dip without fear of wetting the feet of any passengers. Underbody shielding is also impressive here – although it is sensible to exercise caution with ground clearance since it is easier to get a longer wheelbase Vitara 'beached' than its more nimble short relative. But that is not to say that owners of this model should hold back in any way.

Off-roading with an automatic gearbox need not cause any problems since you can still hold the transmission in **Low** first – and that is usually where you need it most. As with other Vitara models, the multi-valve, high-revving characteristics of the engine certainly limit the vehicle's engine braking ability and a dab of left foot braking can help to ease the machine down particularly steep slopes. A good driver will get to know the transmission before attempting anything too demanding. Obviously, you do not just leave the transmission in Drive as you might on the road since slippery surfaces and

Thankfully, when the five-door was introduced it did not appear as a sort of small Transit van with wheelarches. The shape carries the Vitara theme well.

wheel spin could have the poor transmission changing up and down the ratios without knowing what was going on – the same of which could be said of the driver!

The five-door Vitara has certainly opened up the range to a brand-new market. In many respects it is a completely different vehicle from the Sport model tested here. If one is most definitely for the young-at-heart looking for a fun vehicle, the five-door can be said to be rather more practical, like a good pair of sensible shoes. The important point, of course, is that underneath they are very similar. The five-door can be just as much fun if you take it off-road and is certainly still a vehicle with a lot of young-at-heart style. And when the weather turns really nasty there will be a lot of motorists who will turn with envy at the very practical nature of the Vitara five-door. I think that is the motoring equivalent of having your cake and eating it, isn't it?

Choosing secondhand

What to look out for

At the time of writing, exactly six years after the European launch in Edinburgh, Suzuki GB plc have sold some 30,000 Vitaras. That's an impressive figure for such a specialist multi-purpose vehicle, especially when you look at the more recent trends of the UK motor industry, which during the early Nineties has witnessed a significant drop in new car registrations.

However, four-wheel drive vehicles in general have been seen to buck this trend, one of the reasons being that people are actually moving over to these vehicles from 'normal' cars. So, whereas a family with two children – and probably a dog! – might in the past have considered an Estate car of some sort, the Vitara five-door now becomes an interesting option.

Similarly, the 'hot hatch' GTi phenomenon of the Eighties has all but died, finally kicked into touch with the boot of increasing insurance premiums, and many of those potential owners now enjoy their motoring at a slightly less frenetic pace, behind the wheel of a specially equipped three-door Vitara. Unfortunately, insurance companies are beginning to turn their grizzled attention towards four-wheel drives, although at present the demand still remains high.

Of course, the secondhand market's strength is a good thing when you are a proud owner, but not quite so good if you are a prospective one. With new Vitara sales strong, and owners enjoying their vehicles to the full, there are limited numbers available in the secondhand market and prices can be correspondingly high. Indeed, this has even led to Suzuki dealers buying vehicles that are for sale from private advertisements so that they can keep a good secondhand stock on their forecourts!

It must also be remembered that few dealers ever sell a 'standard' Vitara. Part of the enthusiasm for the vehicle is the fact that owners are able to personalize each one with a variety of accessories. If you are looking for a secondhand vehicle, therefore, when you look at two models of the same specification and year, they could be very different – as could the prices being asked.

Suzuki GB plc's technical managers are keen to stress that the vehicle must be serviced regularly (covered in more detail in the fifth chapter). Therefore, it is sensible when buying secondhand to examine closely the service history of the vehicle. The philosophy behind Suzuki's desire to see the vehicle regularly is *not* prompted by its having any particularly weak areas, but

When buying a secondhand Vitara, you have a variety of options depending on what the original owner decided when he or she bought the vehicle. You could find a relatively standard machine, one that has had a particularly sporting life or one that has received a certain amount of cosmetic surgery and 'grown' wheelarch extensions, great big fat wheels and tyres. Whatever the case, your checklist of points to examine should be much the same.

simply because the Vitara is a multi-purpose vehicle. If it has been taken off-road, it has been put under far greater stress than 'normal' vehicles. Suzuki, however, do not have two different levels of servicing for those Vitaras taken off-road and those that live life firmly on the tarmac, as that would be impossible to monitor. Therefore, it is assumed that every Vitara has been taken off-road and must consequently go through a vigorous checking procedure at every service – something that is worth much peace of mind when buying secondhand.

One of your first questions to a prospective vendor is going to be, "Has the vehicle been taken off-road?". For many people, a shake of the head followed

Under the bonnet, make sure you check the oil in the transmission to see if there is any water contamination.

Check the conditions of all exposed electrical leads, especially if the vehicle has spent time off-road.

A Vitara that has been 'jumped' off-road can show signs of damage around the top of the front struts. If this is the case, take care since repair could prove expensive.

by: "Oh no, never" might seem the better answer. Personally, I would rather find an enthusiastic owner who has used the vehicle as it was designed. Certainly, you should have little to worry about with a well looked after, regularly serviced and regularly off-roaded, Vitara.

You will, of course, be able to answer the off-road question yourself, by getting down on your hands and knees and having a really thorough look underneath, for it is here that the scars of the off-road battlefield will be seen. The relative lack of ground clearance – it's only eight inches after all – will mean the vehicle's crossmember is likely to carry some marks and dents. However, much of the underbody components are shielded and sensible off-roading will not have caused more than a few scuffs and scratches.

Nonetheless, it is possible to damage the front suspension turrets if you 'jump' a Vitara off-road. So check under the bonnet, around the top of the suspension turrets for any obvious damage, although to be absolutely sure, expert inspection would be required. The safest thing here is not to buy any Vitara that looks as though it has had a particularly hard thump, up through the front suspension.

One particularly good tip that was given by Mike McNulty, Suzuki GB plc's Technical Training Manager, is to whip out the oil level plug from the transfer 'box. All you are looking for here is to see whether the oil is particularly badly discoloured or worse still, whether it has emulsified showing it to be contaminated with water. The Vitara is designed to wade through water up to the bottom of the doors, but if it has gone deeper – or the driver has failed to

The interior of the Vitara is relatively hard-wearing and so a well-looked after vehicle should still be in good condition despite high mileage. Always have a thorough look under the floor foot mats.

Get down on your hands and knees and examine the vehicle's underbelly. If it has been seriously off-roaded, any damage should show up here. The crossmember (pictured) can take quite a pounding, so don't worry about minor dents and thumps.

keep a nice bow wave ahead of the vehicle or has stopped for any reason, allowing that wave to wash back through and under the vehicle – it is possible for water to find its way into the transfer 'box down the breather tube. That in itself is not a great problem, provided the car is well maintained, comprehensively checked after an off-road session and the oil changed. If the oil is not changed, the water will prevent the gears getting the necessary lubrication and since Japanese gears are particularly fine-toothed to keep transmission noise and whine to a minimum, it is likely that they will experience excessive wear or possibly break off the tips. McNulty's advice was to steer clear of any Vitara that has a transfer box contaminated with water since you can never tell just how much damage has already been done.

Once you have given the vehicle a good look over, the next job is to go for a drive, and here the advice is particularly important for newcomers to four-wheel drive. The Vitara should drive and feel like a 'normal' car. The driving position is higher than many will be used to, which is one of the benefits. If the vehicle doesn't have power steering, you may find it a touch on the heavy side – especially if you are driving one with ultra-wide wheels and tyres. You must also remember that this isn't a racing car: the ride should be comfortable, but the handling is different and familiarity does take time. While the novice four-wheel drive owner may feel that the Vitara rolls a little more than he or she is used to, what should not be experienced are any nasty vibrations or strange mechanical noises. The moment your vendor says "Oh, they all do that. It's a four-wheel drive you know", stop the vehicle and politely hand over the keys. You don't want this one.

If the vehicle has free-wheeling hubs fitted, no vibration should be felt when they are set in the FREE position. If a small vibration sets in at 30-50mph – as with any vehicle – that could possibly be an out-of-balance wheel, so check to see if a weight has become dislodged. Vibration around 60-70mph, however, might well be a propshaft problem, and could range from a small unpleasant vibration to the whole car feeling that it is about to fall apart.

A great number of Vitaras are fitted with large wheel and tyre combinations. Suffice to say here that Suzuki GB plc do not recommend the fitting of such wheels and tyres as they can damage the vehicle's suspension and affect warranty claims, so take care. If you are buying a Vitara with enormous 10in wheels from a reputable Suzuki dealer, ask whether all the suspension components and wheel bearings have been checked and how this may affect any secondhand warranty schemes that may be on offer.

While remembering that these vehicles are not racing cars, it is worth commenting that the engines do like to work quite hard. In the case of the later 16v versions, do not be afraid to use the full rev range when driving; the engine should still feel smooth and powerful, if a little noisy, right up to the red line.

The driveline and transmission on the Vitara are well protected. However, don't be afraid to get the underside power-washed to have a good look.

If you are buying one of the earlier carburettor models, these should prove even easier to service at home or could be looked after quite simply by a non-franchised dealer.

The bodywork on all Vitaras, including the early models, should be in reasonable condition. Corrosion should not have taken a hold since much of the bottom half is well protected. Any Vitara that looks particularly tatty has just not been properly looked after. All cars need a certain amount of tender loving care and this one is no exception. Since it is a multi-purpose machine, it needs a little more attention if it is taken off-road and you will soon notice if that has not been the case.

If the vehicle is fitted with a tow hook, check how much towing work it has been doing. It is a tough little machine but it is still a relative lightweight and only has a 1,600cc engine. Towing capacity with a braked trailer is 1,000lb (450kg) for the three-door and 1,500lb (680kg) for the five-door; using an unbraked trailer it is only 1,000lb (450kg) for both. If possible, have a look at what the owner has been towing to ensure he hasn't been driving the workhorse too hard in this department.

If you are looking for an open-topped model, you will obviously take great care to check out the canvas hood. Unfortunately, a great many open-topped vehicles become vandalized so ensure that any damage has been properly repaired. It is probably a good idea to take off the hood and refit it yourself before you make a decision, since that way you check all the fixings. A new soft-top will cost in the region of £340-£450 depending on model and colour

Also, check behind the left-hand rear wheel to see whether the exhaust has been damaged. It is tucked away, but could have taken a thump or two if the vehicle has been driven off-road.

(May 1994 prices) so if the vehicle you are looking at obviously needs a new hood, adjust the price accordingly.

It is not possible to look in any great detail at the prospective prices for the Vitara here, so you should always check out the experts. *Off Road and 4 Wheel Drive* magazine, for example, publishes a secondhand four-wheel drive buyer's guide which includes the Vitara, and this is updated every month. The cheapest Vitara you are likely to find will obviously be a 1988 three-door, carburettor model, which is going to set you back around £4,000. One of the best secondhand buys, if you can find one, is the JLX SE Executive model with its special paintwork, power everything and smart 'Suzuki-approved' alloy wheels. As a rough guide, a two-year-old version will probably cost around £8,500 – which only confirms the extent to which the Vitara is holding its own in the secondhand marketplace.

It may take some time, therefore, but a secondhand Suzuki Vitara could be a promising purchase. It may, perhaps, be a little optimistic to say that it would be an investment, but a Vitara that is a couple of years old will have dropped that initial depreciation to level out. If it has been well looked after, you should consequently be able to get a good price if you decide to sell...but then again, if you are reading this book, you're not going to want to sell, are you?

Looking after your Vitara

Servicing advice

Owning a Suzuki Vitara is different from owning a 'normal' car. The Vitara is a multi-purpose machine capable of taking you and your family on exciting and highly enjoyable drives far away from the oh-so-boring tarmac. It is fair to ask, however, whether there is a penalty to be paid with vastly increased service bills for what is surely a technically highly complex piece of automotive machinery.

The simple answer to this is a resounding "No". You may like to amaze and entertain your friends and colleagues by describing the intricacies of free-wheeling hubs and the gear ratios of your transfer case, but if truth be told, the Suzuki Vitara is a relatively simple vehicle.

And that is one of its major strengths. It has been designed to be sold in a variety of different markets around the world and the last thing that Suzuki want are servicing problems and high warranty claims.

Despite all that, the Vitara is *different* from the 'normal' road car and does therefore require a different sort of service from the average small Japanese hatchback. The reason is obviously because the Vitara has off-road capabilities and, as stated in the previous chapter, the standard Suzuki service procedure takes the very sensible line of assuming that *all* Vitaras are driven off-road.

Suzuki GB plc stress that the Vitara needs to be serviced regularly. This does not mean that they expect problems, but merely that if the Vitara has been driven off-road it needs a number of items checked on a regular basis. In this chapter many of these checks are explained – but not, I hasten to add, so that you avoid taking your Vitara in for regular servicing. Every time the Vitara goes off-road it needs a good clean down afterwards and a careful check over – tasks always best done by the owner.

After that enjoyable day's off-roading, a good blast with a high pressure wash is absolutely necessary. A certain amount of social responsibility is needed here as really muddy four-wheel drives are sometimes banned from garage forecourt power-washing facilities because the cleaning process can block the drains. My advice is to find a friendly local car wash.

Don't forget to clean under the bonnet. The Vitara's engine will stand

SUZUKI

SERVICE CHECK SHEET
VITARA SE416

SERVICE SCHEDULE TICK ON COMPLETION

MODEL. _____

REG No: _____

CUSTOMER: _____

R.O. NO: _____

MTHS/MILES

1	6	12	18	24	30	36	42	48

☐ Check/Adjust ⦿ Replace ■ Not Applicable

Replace oil filter
Replace engine oil (API Grade SG SAE 10w/40)
Check brake fluid (DOT 4 J1703) (Replace every 2 years/24,000 miles)
Inspect propshaft/driveshafts including gaiters
Inspect transmission lubricant levels
Replace transmission lubricants (Auto trans every 3 years/36,000 miles)
Replace oil cooler hoses (Auto trans only)
Inspect P.A.S. fluid level (where applicable)

Inspect water pump belt tension and condition (Replace every 4 years/48,000 miles)
Check and adjust valve clearance
Check engine mounting bolts
Check cylinder head and rocker shaft bolts
Check coolant strength and system for leaks
Replace coolant
Inspect ignition wiring LT and HT leads
Inspect distributor cap and rotor arms
Replace spark plugs (every 6 months/6,000 miles if leaded fuel is used)
Check ignition timing
Check distributor advance (centrifugal and vacuum)
Air filter (Replace every 2 years/24,000 miles)
Inspect carburettor choke system
Check "Idle up"/throttle damper operation and fuel cut solenoid
Lubricate throttle cable and linkage
Inspect fuel tank cap, lines and connections
Replace fuel filter
Adjust idle speed
Check exhaust emissions (cat damage/HEGO sensor/lambda etc)
Inspect crankcase vent hose and PCV valve (if fitted)

Inspect fuel tank breather system
Inspect battery electrolyte level, terminals and S.G.
Adjust clutch free play
Inspect brake discs, pads, drums, shoes - condition and wear
Inspect handbrake lever and cable - operation (adjust if necessary)
Inspect brake pipes and hoses (leaks etc)
Inspect exhaust system and mountings
Inspect tyres and wheels
Check torque of wheel nuts
Inspect free wheel hubs (if fitted)
Inspect dampers/suspension for security and leaks
Inspect steering linkage for wear and security
Inspect A/C operation and change receiver/dryer (every 12 months)

Inspect wiring harness and connections
Check operations of all lights, warning lights, buzzers and horn
Lubricate door hinges
Check operation and security of seat belts
Check windscreen wiper/washer operation and adjustment (top up fluid)

QUALITY CONTROL CHECK
Road test after all service work including brake test
Ensure interior and exterior are free from grease and dirt

Servicing Dealer:

To ensure this vehicle meets all safety and operational requirements, this work will have been performed by a qualified Suzuki Technician, and will have been undertaken in conjunction with the appropriate Technical Information supplied by the Vehicle Manufacturer

Signature of Service Technician

Date

SUZUKI
Caring for Customers

This is a Vitara service schedule. You will see from the list that the Suzuki technician is going to take a fair amount of time checking over your car – irrespective of whether you take it off-road or remain firmly on the tarmac.

It makes sense for you to keep a good check on the oil levels, not forgetting, of course, that there is an engine and a transmission dipstick under the bonnet.

almost any amount of pressure washing as all the delicate computers have been positioned in-board, out of harm's way. The engine is actually difficult to drown with a spray since it has been designed to be washed down. It's really a case of common sense, avoiding directing the full force of the spray gun at any one place for a long period. Care, too, must be taken if you have had an aftermarket alarm system fitted, as it will not react well if water has been sprayed directly into the horn unit. While under the bonnet, always have a good look at the alternator and clear out any mud and grit; careful cleaning here could avoid an expensive replacement part later.

When power-washing the vehicle, you will obviously clean the wheels and tyres as best you can, but it is a good idea to remove them when you are home and thoroughly clean the inside of the wheels. Some forms of mud and dirt can have a particularly unpleasant consistency and may stubbornly adhere themselves to the inside of the wheel. This will dry hard and could certainly unbalance the wheel, so get rid of it. Such cleaning will also allow you time to check to see that you haven't lost a wheel weight. Tyre pressures should be tested and checked both before and after an off-road session as tyres take quite a hammering, after all. It is also worth inspecting the entire circumference of the tyre and removing any unwanted stones that might have wedged their way into the tread. If you have checked your wheels and tyres without actually removing them, spare a couple of minutes ensuring that the wheelnuts are torqued correctly (again, this should be done, before and after

If you take your Vitara off-road, always remember to clean under the bonnet: it's been designed to cope with a good steam clean every now and again.

The Vitara's electrics are well protected; even those that are exposed are placed high enough and out of the way of water and mud, to suit all but the most enthusiastic off-roaders.

After every off-road session, remove the wheels and clean the insides. This is an area where mud can linger and possibly unbalance the wheel.

an off-road session).

When you look at the Vitara's official service check sheet, the main area of concern is stresses and strains that have occurred to the gearing and transmission components. As a rough estimate, an off-road vehicle will tend to do in 6,000 miles what it would take an on-road vehicle 8-9,000 miles to achieve – which is why it needs to be serviced regularly.

It is vitally important that the transmission lubricant level is inspected. This is not something that would be done on every 'normal' road car service, but if a Vitara is taken off-road and driven through water, it is possible for the

If you have had a serious off-road session you must clean out the vehicle's drum brakes. If wet, gritty mud finds its way inside there, the abrasive effect will destroy the Vitara's brakeshoes extremely quickly.

gearbox to fill up. The snorkel breathing device on the top of the gearbox only goes up as high as the bottom of the doors so if you go deeper than that – or if you are not sufficiently experienced and don't keep the nice bow wave running ahead of the vehicle – you can flood the gearbox and this would obviously contaminate the gearbox oil. Poor lubrication will then occur and ultimately this could mean damaged gear teeth.

If your Vitara has power steering, the hydraulic fluid will need regular attention. It is very unlikely that power steering will fail in normal usage, but off-road the hoses can get damaged. The same can be said about ignition wiring as LT and HT leads can get damaged by dirt from off-roading.

The Vitara's air filter is checked on every service and not just because it might be dirty (this will certainly happen if you are doing a lot of driving in dusty areas). Again the problem is that if the vehicle has been wading and the engine compartment has taken a wash of dirty water, you may not have noticed a thing as performance at the time may have seemed totally

You may not like the catalytic convertor, but you must check whether your latest off-road session has damaged it in any way.

unimpaired, but when a wet air filter dries it will just crumble and break down.

Obviously, many of the problems and areas that need the most care and attention are underneath the vehicle where it is most vulnerable. It is possible, for instance, if you 'jump' a Vitara off-road, to damage the front suspension turrets and that's one item that would then require expert inspection. The front chassis crossmember can also come under a great deal of punishment when it goes off-road, although, of course, it is stopping other bits from getting damaged.

Other underside areas to note vary from exhaust and catalyzers being damaged, to crankcase vent hoses becoming blocked. Steering linkages must be thoroughly and regularly checked because they are the lowest point under the vehicle, which can mean that bottom tie rods sometimes get whacked by rocks and errant tree stumps.

One extremely important area to be inspected is the vehicle's braking system. Brakes wear out much faster on off-road vehicles than normal ones because of all the dirt and grit that gets in the system. This can be a serious problem for some less diligent owners and it is not unknown for brake linings that were expected to last 12-15,000 miles, to be shot after only a mere 1,000. Rear brakeshoes will be destroyed if you don't wash out the drums after an off-road session as all the muck that gets in there will just act as an abrasive paste. The same used to be true of SJ clutches because there was an inspection hole in the bellhousing that quite often lost its rubber seal cover causing the bellhousing to fill up with muck and grit, thus quickly depriving its owner of a clutch. Thankfully, this is not the case with the Vitara.

At first glance, all these points may seem like something of an awesome list and mean that the Vitara is going to set you back with some enormous service bills. This, as stated above, is not the case. Most of what has been described here involves checking and inspecting, something that every good owner should do regularly. The expense will only come when you don't bother to check whether you have water in the transmission and are told you need a replacement as a result. That's when it hurts most.

Getting personal

Accessories for your Vitara

Your car is an extension of your personality, or so it's often said. In that case, Vitara owners are a weird and wonderful bunch!

Seriously, one of the major attractions of the Vitara is an owner's ability to personalize his or her vehicle, to make a statement. This is an attraction that is positively directed by Suzuki GB plc as Marketing Director, Ian Catford,

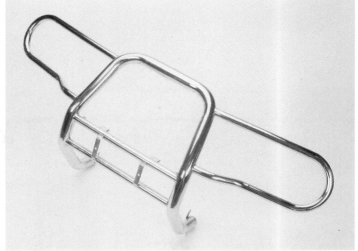

The bull bar is probably – and rightly – the most popular of all Vitara accessories, the vehicle looking almost naked without one. The range of options for your Vitara is tremendous and will depend on how tough you want the vehicle to look, from the simple centre-hooped bar to the full face-saver.

admits: "We don't sell a standard car [as] people's natural instinct is always to add something. The Suzuki philosophy has always been to offer a whole range of accessories which gives people the opportunity to personalize the vehicle. It's far more than just a four-wheel drive vehicle: the Vitara is a fashion statement and that's all to do with image."

Suzuki GB plc boast an extensive list of official Vitara accessories ranging from the highly practical to the highly personal. Add to that the many aftermarket accessory companies who have products for the Vitara and this is one vehicle where you can confidently predict accommodation of everyone's tastes.

There are two major areas where this is especially true: exterior bull bars and styling; and wide wheels and tyres. To take the first, the very name 'bull bar' conveys a pretty tough, macho, approach to life and fitted to the front of a Vitara it certainly looks the business. At the time of writing, however, bull bars have become a particularly controversial subject with some campaigning groups claiming them to be dangerous to pedestrians and other road users.

Suzuki GB plc take an understandably strong and pragmatic line in this argument. Ian Catford: "All our accessories meet the current standards and regulations of the moment. If those regulations were to change, then we would change too. This is especially true with the bull bars which have changed. If there is a demand from the public to alter them further, then that's what we will do. The bars are now much less aggressive, more rounded than

This particular bull bar is fitted for a purpose rather than just for show. If you spend a lot of time off-road, a bar with integral grilles to protect the lights is a good idea.

before. Suzuki is looking at a softer bar as well. Accessory development for the Vitara is an ongoing area."

Whatever the reason, the more recent move to a design that follows the contours of the vehicle rather than one that just stands upright, has to be applauded. Not only are they obviously less likely to cause problems for pedestrians and road users, but they also look considerably more attractive. Yet are they actually necessary, and do they offer any positive benefit for the Vitara owner?

Bull bars, kangaroo bars or cow catchers have a very practical use if you live somewhere like the Australian outback, regularly cross vast rural areas of bush land and have to dodge a variety of wildlife that has yet to master the Highway Code and insists on rushing out in front of you at great speed. In this instance, a bull bar can prevent damage to the vehicle and a possible major accident. Of course, cruising around a UK town looking for a parking space at Tesco on a Saturday does have its difficulties, but marauding wildlife is unlikely to be one of them. For many owners, though, bull bars just look great. Looking through the official Suzuki GB plc catalogue, however, it is obvious that some of the designs would also be useful if you are taking your Vitara off-road.

Off-road driving is relatively simple and a great deal of fun. Done properly, there will be no risk to the occupants and very little to the vehicle. The most likely damage is going to be minor – like a rogue bush or tree branch swinging into the vehicle and breaking headlights or spotlights. Some of the best Vitara bull bars, therefore, are the ones that cover the lights and you will feel far more comfortable when driving down a particularly overgrown green lane, knowing that the bull bar is offering a fair degree of protection.

For the off-roading Vitara owner a bull bar that has the additional front

For those who like something soft on their bonnets...no, that's not what I mean – some accessory companies offer plastic rather than metal bull bars, which are colour-coded to match – or not – depending on your taste!

undercover protector set makes a lot of sense, as does the fitting of side bars. Again, they not only look good, but also offer protection should you find yourself sliding sideways towards a tree – and it is far better that this should take the impact rather than the more flimsy door skin.

Wide wheels and tyres are an equally controversial subject, and you should note Suzuki GB plc's comments in the second chapter. Of course, it all comes down to personal taste, and the aftermarket for wheels and tyres is enormous. It is also worth thinking hard before you decide on what you intend doing with your Vitara. Wide wheels and tyres on a car without power steering will make parking a muscle-aching operation, the vehicle's off-road ability could be seriously hampered, and if you live in a part of the country that gets covered with snow, you'll be leaving the Vitara at home – which seems something of a waste. Fitting some smart alloy wheels that keep the standard wheel and tyre size seems a good compromise, but this is just a personal opinion.

Protective side bars are a popular choice and do have a beneficial effect when off-roading since they can stop you denting a door when sliding gracefully into a tree.

Cover that spare wheel with something that suits your personality – if you like jigsaws, for instance....

If you never have any back-seat passengers in your Vitara Sport, why not consider the Sprint version of the soft-top, available in a variety of colours?

You can get quite personal, too, when considering colour schemes for Vitaras. There are now a great variety of replacement soft-tops in some exciting colours including salmon, mint and, would you believe, orchid? These are available in the standard shape or as the Sprint soft-top which gives the Vitara a coupé look but is only suitable if it remains a two-seater. Matched with these are the spare-wheel covers which allow for some interesting graphics, the standard Suzuki GB plc versions being rather tame compared with what is available in the aftermarket.

On the more practical side, those people who use their Vitaras for towing and touring are equally well catered for. Attractive, quality luggage racks can be purchased for both the three and five-door models, and there is even a luggage rack available with a large rear upper spoiler, although quite what aerodynamic effect this will have when you are using the roof rack is questionable – so perhaps if it is not in use, it would be better to remove it altogether. For those who use their Vitaras for adventurous weekend activities, luggage rack adapters for skis, surf and sailboards and mountain bikes are additionally available.

These weekend activities are also the occasions when the vehicle can get particularly wet and dirty, inside as well as out, and this is where some internal protection should be considered. There are hard-wearing footwell mats available, including those that are custom-made to fit in the rear luggage compartment. Better still, if you carry a lot of bits and pieces with you, are the moulded plastic liners that offer excellent protection for interior carpets, which are ideal when taking all the garden rubbish down to the dump.

A set of vinyl seat covers would also be a sensible purchase for those taking the vehicle off-road regularly, as being very functional they offer important

For those who want to keep really warm when the winter arrives, a hardtop is available, turning the Sport into a fully enclosed three-door Vitara.

You can increase the
carrying capacity of both
three and five-door Vitaras
with a variety of options.

One of the best ways to keep the interior of your Vitara undamaged is to have a tough, plastic liner for the rear – ideal, for example, when taking garden refuse down to the local rubbish dump.

If you regularly carry loose objects in the rear – and I don't just mean of the canine variety - a guard makes a great deal of sense.

protection for the upholstery.

As far as keeping things tidy, there are centre armrest consoles (for five-door models), tidy box sets, neat rear pockets that can be fitted to estate models and the all-important lockable security box. This is a must for all soft-top Vitara owners because, let's face it, a vehicle with a hood is never totally secure. The box bolts away out of view and is big enough to take the removable radio cassette player, wallets, passports etc. This should be top of anyone's accessory list if they own a Vitara Sport.

Probably one item that fewer owners would consider is a set of **free-wheeling hubs** – which may well be because they don't understand what they are or how they work. This, actually simple, enhancement has been covered in the technical chapter, but its function is well worth reiterating here: the Vitara's four-wheel drive system is part-time, and in normal road use the engine is turning only the rear wheels. Move the 'other' gear-lever – the transfer lever – into the four-wheel drive position and the engine will turn all four wheels. When you are in two-wheel drive, however, the front wheels still turn the front driveshafts, front differential and front propshaft. A certain

This carry-all tidy bag means there really is no excuse to have items rolling around cluttering your Vitara.

amount of effort is needed to do this and that effort involves more fuel, which means more expense. Free-wheeling hubs disconnect the front wheels and allow them to 'wheel freely', so less effort is needed and therefore you will use less fuel. The vehicle will also run more smoothly on the road with free-wheeling hubs as well as having a slightly lower transmission noise. For Vitara owners doing the majority of their miles on-road, this option makes a lot of sense.

There are two varieties of free-wheeling hubs: those that have to be twisted manually before you get four-wheel drive; and the more expensive, but much more practical, automatic versions that engage as you select four-wheel drive and are disengaged by reversing the vehicle a couple of yards when you have finished off-roading.

Items like free-wheeling hubs are obviously best bought direct through Suzuki GB plc, but if you are interested in exterior styling items you can certainly look further afield. Bonx offer a range of dramatic styling accessories for the Vitara. Best known for their brightly coloured front bars, Bonx also have body kits, side bars and spoilers on offer; their bull bars are actually made from 'soft' plastic – designed for their looks not structural practicality. For those keen on personalizing the Vitara's interior there are Walnut trim kits, 'designer sports' dashboard, leather steering wheels and even fully tailored leather upholstery. Bonx can be contacted on Tel: 01373 831344; Fax: 01373 831190.

Trans Atlantic 4x4 probably have one of the most extensive ranges of wheels available for the Vitara. However, you should take time to consider not just how wide you will go, but also which wheels will look the best because it is easy to spend a lot of money in this area of styling. Trans Atlantic 4x4 can be contacted on Tel: 01773 540910; Fax: 01773 540752.

Official Suzuki Vitara Accessories

VITARA THREE-DOOR

Part No:	Description
Exterior styling	
99000-990YB-100	Centre bull bar set
99000-990YB-116	Front under cover set
99000-990YB-167	Front mudflap set
99000-990YB-170	Rear mudflap set
99000-99069-155	Rear bumper cover
99000-990YB-210	Rear wash/wipe
99000-990YB-360	Hardtop – white
99000-990YB-361	Hardtop – black
99000-990YB-291	Side bull bar set
99000-990YB-296	Side bull bar set with lamp provision
99006-80831	Side sill bar - black
99006-80831-00W	Side sill bar - white
99006-84006	Side sill step set - black
99006-84006-00W	Side sill step set - white
99006-84008-00S	Side steps - stainless steel
99006-83002	Standard bull bar - black
99006-83002-00W	Standard bull bar - white
99006-83100-0SS	A shape bull bar - stainless steel
99006-83102-0SS	A shape bull bar with brushguards stainless steel
99006-83106	Tubular bull bar - black
99006-83106-00W	Tubular bull bar - white
99006-83010	Front under cover set
99006-83042	Canvas bikini top

99006-57762-03	Sun port soft-top - salmon
99006-57762-06	Sun port soft-top - mint
99006-57762-09	Sun port soft-top - charcoal
99006-557762-15	Sun port soft-top - black denim
99006-57762-52	Sun port soft-top - white denim
99006-57762-53	Sun port soft-top - red
99006-57762-55	Sun port soft-top - orchid
99006-57762-57	Sun port soft-top - yellow
99006-57172-03	Replacement soft-top - salmon
99006-57172-06	Replacement soft-top - mint
99006-57172-09	Replacement soft-top - charcoal
99006-57172-15	Replacement soft-top - black denim
99006-57172-52	Replacement soft-top - white denim
99006-57172-53	Replacement soft-top - red
99006-57172-55	Replacement soft-top - orchid
99006-57172-57	Replacement soft-top - yellow
99006-57372-003	Sprint soft-top - salmon
99006-57372-06	Sprint soft-top - mint
99006-57372-09	Sprint soft-top - charcoal
99006-57372-15	Sprint soft-top black - denim
99006-57272-52	Sprint soft-top - white denim
99006-57372-53	Sprint soft-top - red
99006-57372-55	Sprint soft-top - orchid
99006-573722-57	Sprint soft-top - yellow
99006-83410	Verdi wheel cover
99006-83420	Rossini wheel cover
99006-83430	'4WD' spare-wheel cover - grey
99006-83440	Multi-coloured spare-wheel cover - white
99006-83450	'Sport' spare-wheel cover - black
99006-83460	'Sport' spare-wheel cover - white
99006-83470	Jigsaw wheel cover - black
99006-83480	Jigsaw wheel cover - white
99000-990YB-330	Hard spare-wheel case - grey
99000-99024-E00	Side protection moulding
99000-990YB-120	Fender arch moulding set
99000-990YB-128	Wheeltrim set (steel wheel)
99000-99069-195	Muffler end piece
99000-990YB-352	Chrome grille
99006-Stripe	Chrome stripe
99001-83810	Locking wheelnut set
99006-Chameleon	6in alloy wheel
99006-Sahara	6in alloy wheel

Towing & Touring

99000-990YB-134	Soft-top roof rack
99000-990YB-139	Hardtop roof rack
99000-990YB-145	Ski rack module
99000-990YB-146	Bicycle rack module
99000-990YB-147	Surf/sail module
99000-990YB-148	Luggage rack soft-top
99000-990YB-149	Luggage rack hardtop
99001-80880	Tow ball kit
99001-80890	Electrics kit
99006-80060	Tow bar
99000-99034-418	Rear gate pocket
99000-99069-155	Rear bumper cover
99000-990YB-181	Rear upper spoiler soft
99000-990YB-183	Rear upper spoiler
43800-60811	Manual free-wheel hub (each)
99000-99080-100	Auto free-wheel hub set
99006-80001	Dash tidy

Instrumentation & Lighting

99000-99042-420	Voltmeter
99000-99053-SE3	Altimeter/inclinometer
99000-990YB-320	Driving light set
99000-990YB-322	Foglamp set
99000-990YB-118	Foglamp holder set
99006-99220	Hella driving-lamp set
99006-9920	Hella 1000 spotlight set
99000-99022-402	Interior lamp delay timer set
99006-99000	Hand-held searchlamp

Interior styling

99000-99004-41E	Rubber floor mat set
99000-99004-78K	Luggage area mat
99000-99023-529	Tray mat set
99006-80850	Logo carpet mat set
99006-83118	Vinyl front seat cover set
99006-83131	Seat cover set - grey
99006-83260	Load liner set
99006-84004	Dog barrier
99006-84002	Vitara two-seater dog guard
99000-99004-53T	Sill cover set

99000-99023-402	Dust box set
99006-85000	Security box bracket
99006-85010	Security box
Sport-Seat-Kit	Sport rear seats kit
99006-82000	Sport rear soundproofing
99006-82010	Sport rear carpet mat
99006-82020	Sport rear rubber mat

VITARA FIVE-DOOR

Exterior styling

99000-990YB-315	Centre bull bar set
99000-990YB-314	Front under cover set
99000-990YB-167	Front mudflap set
99000-990YB-326	Rear mudflap set
99000-990YB-291	Side bull bar set
99000-990YB-296	Side bull bar set (with lamp provision)
99000-990YB-330	Hard spare-wheel case
99006-830004	Bull bar - black
99006-83004-OOW	Bull bar - white
99006-83108-OSS	A shape bull bar - stainless steel
99006-83110-OSS	A shape bull bar with brushguards - stainless steel
99006-83012	Front underplate
99006-80834	Side sill bar - black
99006-80834-00W	Side sill bar - white
99006-83430	Spare-wheel cover
99006-83440	Multi-coloured spare-wheel cover - white
99006-83450	Sport spare-wheel cover - black
99006-83460	Sport spare-wheel cover - white
99006-83470	Jigsaw wheel cover - black
99006-83480	Jigsaw wheel cover - white
99000-990YB-330	Hard spare-wheel case - grey
99000-99025-EO1	Side protection moulding
99000-99069-195	Muffler end piece
99000-990YB-317	Fender arch moulding set
99006-990YB-352	Chrome grill
99000-99069-191	Rear bumper cover
99000-990YB-128	Wheeltrim set (steel wheel)
99001-83810	Locking wheelnut set
99006-Chameleon	6in alloy wheel
99006-Sahara	6in alloy wheel

Towing & Touring

99000-99034-418	Rear gate pocket
99000-990YB-318	Multi-roof rack
99000-990YB-145	Ski rack module (fit with 99000-990YB-18)
99000-990YB-146	Bike rack module (fit with 99000-990YB-318)
99000-990YB-147	Surf/sailboard (fit with 99000-990YB-318)
99000-990YB-149	Luggage rack (fit with 99000-990YB-318)
99000-99069-191	Rear bumper cover
99000-990YB-183	Rear upper spoiler
99000-99080-100	Auto free-wheel set
43800-60811	Manual free-wheel hub (each)
99006-80060	Tow bar
99001-80880	Tow ball
99001-80890	Electrics kit
99006-80001	Dash tidy

Instrumentation & Lighting

99000-99022-402	Interior lamp delay timer set
99000-99053-SE3	Altimeter/inclinometer (includes housing)
99000-99042-420	Voltmeter
99000-990YB-316	Lamp-holder set
99000-990YB-320	Driving-lamp set (per pair)
99000-990YB-322	Foglamp set (per pair)
99006-99200	Hella 1000 spotlight set
99000-99069-199	Luggage light
99006-99220	Driving lamps
99006-99000	Hand-held searchlamp

Interior styling

99000-99004-41N	Rubber floor mat set
99000-99023-402	Dust box set
99000-99023-529	Tray mat set
99000-99004-89Y	Luggage area mat
99006-80854	Carpet mat set
99006-83270	Load liner - half
99006-83280	Load liner - full
99006-84005	Dog barrier
99980-71100	Centre armrest
99006-85005	Security box bracket
99006-85010	Security box
99006-80002	Rear shelf
99001-S3500-Kit	Shelf speaker kit

Taking to the rough stuff

Off-roading your Vitara

Suzuki have changed the face of off-road driving in the UK. While this may sound like a particularly exaggerated statement, it is, nonetheless, one that well withstands investigation.

Back in March 1979, Suzuki GB launched the LJ range to the public,

supporting this with an advertising campaign for "The Wild Weekender". It was a bold and clever move since it gave the LJ a completely new image. This simple, utilitarian 'little jeep' was a very basic vehicle yet it offered its owners the chance to switch to four-wheel drive and take to the rough stuff as a weekend leisure activity – something that had previously been the domain of the dedicated Land Rover enthusiast. The point was, however, that you didn't have to be a completely dedicated off-road enthusiast, nor possess any deep mechanical skill to enjoy four-wheel driving. With the LJ range, Suzuki began to destroy the myth that driving off-road was difficult and only for the experts.

Of course, the LJ's basic nature and levels of equipment were not to everyone's taste, but it was an ideal platform upon which to introduce the SJ series. Longer and wider, with a wheelbase stretched a further four inches, the SJ retained the rugged jeep body style but neatly brought it forward to look

If you own a Vitara, you really must take it off-road. The vehicle is tough and has been designed to be driven in these kinds of conditions. Off-road driving is fun, and it's a family sport.

Prospective Grand Prix racers stop here – and go away: off-road driving is not about high speed and jumping wheels.

rather less out-of-place on the road. The SJ series developed in a number of directions, the most important being the burgeoning leisure market.

With its bright and cheeky paint schemes, bull bars and fancy wheels, the SJ series went down a storm during the prosperous Eighties, gaining particular acceptance in the 'Yuppie' world; indeed, who would have thought such a vehicle would be seen by many as actually more *chic* than a Golf GTi? The SJ's advantage, you see, was that it had four-wheel drive and could be driven off-road.

Suzuki GB plc developed this off-road enthusiasm through the **Rhino Club** (see next chapter) and many thousands of people started off-roading, discovering very quickly the two most important facts: it's fun and it's very easy to learn.

The change of image and emphasis that has been put on the Vitara since the SJ range is discussed elsewhere, but how does this translate to off-road driving?

It is fair to say that the Suzuki SJ looks as though it should be driven off-road. Its tough, jeep-like appearance suggests a sort of 'it-doesn't-matter-if-it-gets-dirty' approach. You can even take that one step further by saying that maybe it doesn't matter if it acquired the odd scratch or dent, but the Vitara is surely completely different.

The Vitara's success has been based on its good looks, and for some new owners who have perhaps never enjoyed off-road driving, those good looks are too good to risk. This would be an understandable, but incorrect conclusion. The Vitara is an ideal enthusiast's off-roader that can give a great deal of enjoyment away from the tarmac.

Although it should have always been expected, given the reputation of the SJ, the Vitara has surprised many a motoring journalist with its off-road ability. If you read any of the group tests that occur in the motoring magazines, such as the annual 4x4 Of The Year Group Test in *Off Road & 4 Wheel Drive*, you

In Low ratio four-wheel drive, with your free-wheeling hubs locked (if fitted, see text) the Vitara will cope with pretty tough terrain.

will see just how well the Vitara matches up off-road with what you might consider to be more illustrious – and certainly more expensive – competitors.

Off-roading is very different from normal driving, but you must not be worried that different also means difficult. Following some simple rules, and with very little actual hands-on experience, most people can become very competent off-roaders.

The first step off the public road should be to ensure that you know your vehicle. This may seem very obvious, but it is actually essential and well worth particular attention. Before venturing off, for instance, be sure you are aware of the vehicle's bodywork, both ahead of and behind the axles. In the case of the Vitara there is little front or rear overhang which gives it good approach and departure angles. Look underneath your vehicle to check where the protective guards are positioned. These will help when you venture into the rough stuff, but it is useful to remember this when trying to avoid awkward rocks, tree stumps or roots.

If you have passengers, encourage them to belt up! Seat belts are not a legal requirement if you are driving on private land but they are simply a must. Ensure everyone has their arms inside and not leaning out of the windows; despite any problems during hot weather, having the windows closed is actually the best bet. This is not only safer should you get into difficulty and roll your car, but it also avoids problems if you encounter any wayward tree branches or bushes brushing alongside the vehicle.

From behind the wheel, all you need to do is engage four-wheel drive. Regular road driving will have the second transmission lever firmly in **2H**, which is **two-wheel drive High** ratio. Move the lever to **4H** and you have **four-wheel drive High** ratio, which you would use for slippery road driving, during a snowy winter for instance. What I am describing here, however, is *proper* off-roading and for this you need **4L**: four-wheel drive **Low** ratio. You have now connected the engine's drive to all four wheels through the transfer case giving you a whole new set of gearbox ratios that are much lower than the normal road ones, allowing you to crawl up and down difficult terrain without having to slip the clutch.

Speed is a very important medium to understand when off-roading. The best off-road drivers have very sensitive right feet, offering 'just enough' throttle to the engine to do the job, but not too much so that you spin wheels and hurl mud and rocks everywhere. Spinning wheels are undesirable since this is likely to create more problems than it solves. It is all a question of balance because you will need to keep the Suzuki's engine singing since maximum torque is produced around 3,000rpm, but this will come with experience.

Although you may spend much of the time at a relatively slow speed of perhaps 10-15mph, it is still very important to look ahead and plan your route. Off-road, positioning your car is far more important than it would be on a normal road and placing the car one foot to the left or right could mean the difference between an easy passage or getting completely stuck. If the going is particularly tricky, good off-roaders will actually get out and have a look at the terrain ahead. This is obviously most important when cresting any hills, for instance, so that you know what is on the other side before you

The Vitara has relatively good Approach and Departure angles, shown in the drawings and demonstrated in the photograph with the driver approaching and climbing the rough stuff. The driver in question is a very serious-looking Brian Hartley, who actually taught this book's author a great deal about off-road driving for which I am very grateful. Brian now runs Club Off Road (address at end of chapter) where he will do the same for new Vitara owners. Oh, and he smiles while he's doing it usually...

actually arrive there. Alternatively, if you are approaching a steep ascent that may demand some extra momentum to get you up, do you know what you are going to find when you get to the top?

Your sensitive right foot should be matched with equally sensitive movement of the steering wheel. Don't hold it in a vice-like grip because when driving off-road the wheel will move around quite a lot on its own as the front wheels traverse the uneven surfaces. You must not *fight* the wheel and make sure you keep your thumbs on the top of the rim, not hooked around the spoke as you might in normal road conditions. This is because you are likely to have numerous occasions when the front wheels will hit a rut or boulder and violently jerk the steering wheel – which can be very painful if it takes your thumb with it; broken fingers can be the result.

In really muddy and slippery conditions you will soon see how sensitive you need to be since simply yanking the wheel one way may have no effect at all in changing the vehicle's direction. Your front wheels may have very little grip to change the direction immediately, while your four-wheel drive system may still have enough traction to move you forward. It is sometimes a case of coaxing the front of the car into a new direction and getting the front wheels straight as soon as possible so that progress can then resume in your chosen direction.

The downhill direction is always the most impressive when driving off-road. On particularly steep declines, again it is always a good idea to have a look first. When you are satisfied that it is safe and that it's where you want to go,

How not to enter the water. The idea is not to make a great splash but rather to ease the vehicle into the water at a moderate speed so as to keep a bow wave ahead of the machine all the way through the obstacle.

If you are worried about off-roading your Vitara, why not try one of the off-road centres listed at the end of this chapter?

check that you are in **Low** first gear and gently drive over the edge, making sure your feet are away from all the pedals! It is really a case of letting the Vitara do all the work. On all but the steepest slopes, the engine will be able to turn the wheels so slowly that you simply crawl down. On steeper slopes, the lack of engine braking available may mean that a dab on the brakes is called for if you feel you are going down too fast, but make sure that you do not stamp on the brakes since in slippery conditions it can be only too easy to lock up the wheels – which will mean that you will 'toboggan' down the slope out of control. Have faith in the vehicle, try some simple slopes first and you will soon get the hang of it. *Never* declutch on a downhill slope since that stops the drive to all four wheels and you will have no control over the speed of your descent, which is both dangerous and potentially expensive.

However, it is fair to comment that the Vitara's engine braking ability is not really that great. The best engines for this particular manoeuvre are lusty V8s with a great deal of torque. Small multi-valve units that work best at high revs are not ideal, but for most off-road adventures the Vitara can be coaxed to work pretty well indeed.

Once down the other side, you may now want to go up with the Vitara, but you will need to muster some enthusiasm from the engine. Remember that the little 1,600cc unit only has 74bhp, so it is likely that you will need some momentum. Second or third gear **Low** range will be necessary for most slopes and you will probably be able to judge the speed depending on the steepness. You must try to ease right off the accelerator as you reach the top of the slope as this will prevent the front of the car 'jumping' in the air when it gets to this point – something that may look dramatic but can be uncomfortable for the occupants and potentially damaging for the vehicle. You also need to be in control at the very top to plan where exactly you are going next – with the front wheels four feet in the air, you'll be staring at the sky which makes it unlikely that you will even see where you are going to land!

The biggest off-road problems occur when you run out of steam half way up a hill. If it is not too steep an ascent, nor the conditions too slippery, you should be able to apply the handbrake and hold yourself in position while you collect your thoughts. But if it ain't going up, it's going to have to go down. *Never* try to turn round and traverse a hill from this position – that could prove to be a serious mistake. You are just going to have to return the way you came, but this time in Reverse gear. Once again this means that you must follow the same rules as before: select the right gear – this time **Reverse Low** ratio – take your feet off everything and let the vehicle take you back down. It is a touch daunting the first time you try, but it impresses the passengers!

It is worth learning a **backward stall start** here since this will avoid the need for you to balance letting out the clutch and releasing the handbrake while simultaneously looking over your shoulder and trying to steer down a hill. Much simpler is to turn the engine off – in truth you may even have stalled the engine trying to climb the hill – ensure that the ignition is on, and then select reverse and release the handbrake. As you move off, the engine will

After your off-road session, always check that the engine's electrics are clean and tidy.

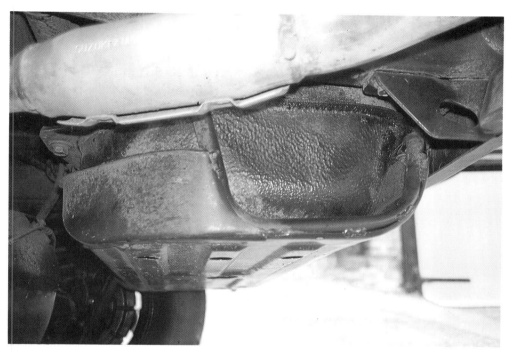

As has been explained earlier in this book, the Vitara has a good level of underbody protection to encourage its off-road use. This is the shield to the rear fuel tank.

restart and you will chug slowly back down.

In really difficult and slippery conditions, failing to get up a slope might mean that you have to act rather quickly, especially if the handbrake fails to hold you. In that case you need to be able to use the backward stall technique smoothly and rapidly. It's something that is easy to practise on the right hill. Drive halfway up, deliberately stall the engine and then swiftly engage Reverse and return down the slope. You'll master it quite quickly and it will certainly come in useful.

When off-roading, it's quite likely that you will be following established tracks. These could well have developed into quite deep ruts, but provided there is enough ground clearance, your Vitara will follow these ruts rather like a train on a track. However, there will be times when you need to check that the centre part of the track will clear under the vehicle. Failure to recognize this could lead to you 'beaching' the underbelly of the car with all four wheels unable to get any grip.

When crossing ruts, make sure you do so at a slight angle, *never* directly at 90 degrees to the rut. The ideal approach is to put just one front wheel into the rut first, followed by a second wheel as the first drives out. The axle articulation on the Vitara is pretty good, thanks to the coil spring suspension,

Power-wash under the vehicle and get rid of all the mud; that way you can check for any damage. Driven properly, however, the Vitara will certainly take more punishment than most owners will throw at it.

so within reason you are unlikely to have much of a problem here.

Another fun part of off-roading is driving through water. Here it certainly pays to have some advance knowledge, such as knowing exactly how deep it is, for instance! If you are driving on an approved course or site, water crossing should not prove a problem. Again speed, or rather the lack of it, is the only major area to master. Beginners often tend to approach water far too quickly which can damage the vehicle's electrics. Instead the Vitara should be eased into the water and then driven through at a speed that keeps a nice bow wave ahead of the bonnet. Don't stop in the middle to admire the view since you can never tell if you will get going again. You'll also be pleased to remember that the Vitara has a number of galvanized parts underneath that smart body shell so you don't need to worry about them getting wet, although a thorough power wash is always to be recommended after any off-road

Take your Vitara off-road and it will get muddy – and never mind anything you do to try to stop it, the inside will get muddy too! Suzuki GB have some excellent, highly recommended protective seat covers for the Vitara.

activity, especially to the vehicle's underside.

It would take a separate book to cover the importance of wheels and tyres to off-roading, so here are just some necessary words of advice to Vitara owners who have a gorgeous set of alloy wheels with super wide road tyres. These, as previously discussed, are not the best items for off-roading and are more likely to land you in difficulties than the standard Vitara fitments. Also alloy wheels are relatively 'soft' and will easily get damaged on rocks and stones, so watch out where you are driving. Vitaras perform very well on standard road tyres, but if you wanted to get serious about this off-roading lark, buying a second set of wheels and fitting them with **M+S** (Mud and Snow) off-road tyres would be a wise investment.

It is all very well knowing how to drive off-road, but the real question is "Where can I go off-roading?". It is still possible to drive down what are called 'green lanes', but these are not easy to identify and can lead you into problems. To find out where they are it is necessary for you to contact your local Highways department to see which tracks have vehicular Rights of Way.

You should never go off-roading completely alone for the simple reason that if you ever get stuck it helps to have someone to tow you out. Wherever you go, it is a good idea to have a standard off-road accessory 'kit' in the back, comprising a shovel, strong tow rope, decent vehicle jack and a First Aid kit (the latter item is far more likely to be necessary for simple things like insect stings due to the rural nature of the location rather than the possibility of having an accident. However, if you do suffer a more serious problem, having a good First Aid kit and knowing how to use it could prove vital).

Probably the best way to enjoy off-roading is to join a club, and in the case of the Vitara you should try the **Rhino Club** (explained in the following chapter) or go to an off-road school or centre. There are now a great many of these throughout the country where you can join like-minded off-roaders safe in the knowledge that if you do get into difficulties, there will be somebody to help you out.

If you own a Vitara, but have never ventured off into the wilderness, it is well worth considering. A Suzuki Vitara means you like something different, and it gives you the opportunity to go somewhere different with it. The design of tough ladder chassis, coil spring suspension, with good axle articulation all carrying a relatively light body shows that the Vitara has been designed for the rough stuff, so why not take up the challenge and have a go? You'll love it!

Off-Road centres

The following list cannot be used as a recommendation, so always telephone first to find out what is on offer and whether you can use your own vehicle or only those belonging to the school or centre. Further, check to see if the centre offers individual tuition. Costs for courses or driving days also vary greatly, so again confirm these details before you set out. This list was correct at time of writing.

4x4 Drive Off-Road Centre
(The Castle House, Rock Park, Wirral. Tel: 0151 645 8124)
This site near Chester was established in 1993 and covers an area of 90 acres with a claimed 10 miles of green lanes. They have Land Rovers, Haflingers, Quad bikes and Argocats.

The Barony College
(Parkgate, Dumfries. Tel: 01387 86251)
This centre has been established since 1988 and has access to a very large off-road area. They use mainly Land Rovers and also run courses on off-road maintenance.

Brands Hatch 4x4 Off-Road School
(Longfield, Kent. Tel: 01474 872331)
Established in 1990 this school started using Suzuki SJs – so you should feel at home. Good for beginners but not a particularly 'rural' off-road centre.

David Bowyer's Off-Road Centre
(East Foldhay, Zeal Monachorum, Crediton, Devon. Tel: 01363 82666)
Long-established off-road centre catering for many makes including Ford, Land Rover, Nissan, Suzuki and Vauxhall.

Buckmore Park Off-Road Centre
(Maidstone Road, Chatham, Kent. Tel: 01634 861295)
Using a variety of off-road vehicles, this centre also has Quad bikes and the immensely entertaining Honda Pilot off-roaders.

Canterbury Off-Road Driving Centre
(Rushmore Manor, Hoath, Canterbury, Kent. Tel: 01227 728268)
This centre offers Touring days using your own 4x4, so check and take along the Vitara – or
you can drive Land Rover Defenders and Discoverys.

Cheviot 4x4 Centre
(Yearle Farm, Wooler, Northumberland. Tel: 01668 282287)
Encouraging you to bring your own vehicle, this centre was established in 1992 and covers
some 250 acres.

Club Off-Road
(5 Quarryside Road, Mirfield, West Yorkshire. Tel: 01924 469376)
Run by Brian Hartley, who organizes off-road driving at various sites around the country and
offers driving tuition.

Clyro Court
(The Garrison, Brilley, Whitney on Wye, Hereford. Tel: 014973 357)
Centre uses various 4x4s as well as Quad bikes and Honda Pilots.

Don Coyote
(Lamancha Village, near Edinburgh, Lothian. Tel: 0131 443 2881)
Large area available, the centre uses Land Rovers but does offer tuition and accommodation.

East Midlands 4x4 Training Centre
(Manor Farm, Kneeton Road, East Bridgford, Notts. Tel: 01949 20003)
Established in 1993, various off-road vehicles are available to drive.

Edgehill Shooting Ground
(Nadbury House, Camp Lane, Warmington, Oxon. Tel: 01295 878141)
Established for 12 years, this centre uses Range Rovers and Quad bikes.

Fresh Tracks
(Haultwick Farm, Ware, Herts. Tel: 01920 438758)
Centre runs from large public sites in London, Bristol and Manchester. Uses Suzuki SJs as well
as Land Rovers. Tuition on winching also available.

Frontier Trails
(Home Farm, Cholderton, near Salisbury, Wiltshire. Tel: 01980 54162)
Off-road centre where you bring your own vehicle.

Gotwick Wood Off-Road Centre
(Gotwick Wood Farm, Holtye Road, East Grinstead, East Sussex. Tel: 01342 315504)
Various 4x4s are used in this challenging off-road centre. Tuition in competition driving,
winching and preparations for expeditions.

Graham Clark
(The Steading, Dunkeld House Hotel, Dunkeld, Perthshire. Tel: 01350 728700)
Using Land Rovers, Vauxhall Fronteras and Jeep Cherokees, this centre has access to an
impressive area for off-roading and does offer professional tuition.

Highland Drovers
(Kincardine, Boat of Garten, Speyside. Tel: 01479 831329)
Situated near Aviemore in the Scottish Highlands, the Drovers offer family fun days as well as
professional training. Assorted 4x4s as well as Quad bikes and buggies.

Highland Off-Road Adventure Centre
(New House, Plot 3, Strathnacro, Glenurquart, Invernesshire.)
Four different sites, using buggies, Quad bikes and Argocats.

Ian Wright Off-Road Driving School
(7 Church Row, West Peckham, Maidstone, Kent. Tel: 01622 817509)
Varied site near Haywards Heath offering a range of 4x4s including Nissan Patrols, Land Rover Discoverys and Isuzu Troopers.

Lakeland Safari
(Duddon View, 9 Castle Way, Broughton-in-Furness, Cumbria. Tel: 01229 716943)
Offers extensive green laning, using primarily Land Rovers.

Lakeland Village Off-Road Driving
(Lakeland Village, Newby Bridge, Ulverston, Cumbria. Tel: 015395 30090)
Situated near the Lake District National Park, and uses Land Rovers and Vauxhall Fronteras.

Landcraft
(Top Floor, Plas yn Dre, 23 High Street, Bala, Gwynedd. Tel: 01678 520820)
Established back in 1979, with a large variety of sites available, using assorted 4x4s.

Landwise 4x4 Outdoor Activities
(Rothiemurchus Estate, Aviemore, Invernesshire. Tel: 01479 810858)
Various 4x4s used including a Mini Monster truck. Established 1988.

Leisure Pursuits
(Chartin House, Hammerwood Road, Ashurst Wood, West Sussex. Tel: 01342 825522)
Offering various 4x4s, including military vehicles. Fun days and ladies' days are available.

Llama Off-Road Events
(10 Woodend Place, Tettenhall Wood, Wolverhampton. Tel: 01902 756589)
Various sites used in the Midlands area. Established in 1992.

Manby Showground Performance Driving Centre
(Sunny Oak, Little Cowthorpe, Louth, Lincs. Tel: 01507 604375)
Land Rovers, military vehicles and Quad bikes available on site, plus green lane driving.

Mid Norfolk Off-Road Centre
(Wood Farm, Runhall, Norwich. Tel: 01362 850233)
Established in 1989, uses Land Rovers and Daihatsus.

Moorland Off-Road Adventure Sport
(Park House, Church End, Sheriff Hutton, York. Tel: 01347 878207)
Offers adventure days on the Yorkshire Moors using Suzuki SJs.

Motor Safari
(Treetops, Mold, Clwyd. Tel: 01352 770769)
Organizes various sites across the UK using a variety of 4x4s.

Newton Hill Country Sports
(Newton Hill, Wormit, Fife. Tel: 01382 541460)
Concentrates on using a variety of Land Rovers.

North Herefordshire Off-Road Driving School
(The Vauld, Marden, Herefordshire. Tel: 01568 84372)
Established in 1989 and uses Land Rovers and Suzukis.

North Yorkshire Off-Road Centre
(Bay Ness Farm, Robin Hood's Bay, Whitby, North Yorks. Tel: 01947 880371)
In operation for over 20 years; uses Land Rovers and Quad bikes.

Off-Road Leisure
(Arkwright Road, Wellow Brook, North Industry, Corby, Northants. Tel: 01536 403500)
Uses a variety of 4x4s Quad bikes and buggies.

Off-Road Motivations
(Andover Garden Machinery, Salisbury Road, Andover, Hampshire. Tel: 01264 710113)
Situated on the North Hampshire Downs, includes green lanes and uses Land Rovers and Suzuki SJs.

Pro-Trax
(32 Southfield Road, Gretton, near Corby, Northants. Tel: 01536 770096)
Eight different sites using Land and Range Rovers. Offering tuition on winching.

Red Dragon Off-Road
(18 Ragged Staff, Saundersfoot, Dyfed. Tel: 01834 813917)
Site close to St Clears, using Land and Range Rovers.

Ronnie Dale Off-Road Adventure Driving School
(Whiteburn Farm, Abbey St Bathans, Duns, Berwickshire. Tel: 01361 4244)
Variety of new off-road vehicles. Established 1985. Tuition available.

Spectrum 4x4 Driving Centre
(PO Box 9, Hoyland, Barnsley, South Yorkshire. Tel: 01226 748822)
Three different sites using Land and Range Rovers. Junior driving available.

Tuf Going
(Freightmaster's Estate, Coldharbour Lane, Rainham, Essex. Tel: 01268 764830)
Land Rover vehicles used; novice tuition available.

Tuff Terrains
(Abbeycwmhir, Llandrindod Wells, Powys. Tel: 01597 851551)
Suzuki SJs, Land Rovers and Quad bikes. Site includes green lanes.

Tuf-Trax
(Westerings, Station Road, West Haddon, Northants. Tel: 01788 510575)
Site includes some testing terrain. Uses Land Rovers and Stalwart and Bedford trucks.

Venture Off-Road Centre
(Eastern Grove, Squires Drive, Three Holes, Wisbech, Cambs. Tel: 01945 772270)
Includes roll-over simulator. Land and Range Rovers used.

Weardale Off-Road Centre
(Coves House Farm, Wolsingham. Co Durham. Tel: 01388 527375)
Uses Land and Range Rovers plus Quad bikes and Honda Pilots.

Wild Rovers
(38 Chatsworth Road, Hazel Grove, Stockport. Tel: 0161 449 0725)
Situated near Peak District National Park and includes green lanes.

Join the Club – and save a Rhino

When the SJ410 was to be launched, back in 1982, the British importer received several new accessories from Japan. Included among them were some spare-wheel covers with graphics of a lion, tiger, camel and a rhino.

These were looked at in great detail by Chief Executive, John Norman, and Marketing Director, Ian Catford, and it was the rhino that caught their attention, quickly to be adopted as a stylized logo and used on the press releases for the new vehicle. It is unlikely they realized quite what they were starting.

Tough, but fun looking, the rhino had four legs to match the four-wheel drive of the new SJ410 and so it was thought it could say something about the strength and character of the vehicle.

About a year later, the rhino had become reasonably well established to the

The Rhino emblem that started with the SJ and Santana models was the brain-child of the Suzuki GB marketing department, and led to the company's heavy involvement with the Save A Rhino campaign.

Rhinos are much in
evidence at Rhino Club
rallies, and it is definitely
fun for all the family.

Inflatable Rhinos take a fair amount of wind to blow them up...

point that John Norman started to receive questions about rhino conservation and whether Suzuki would like to become associated with this in some way. Norman decided that it was time to formalize the Suzuki rhino and register it as an official trademark to protect it.

By 1985, things had really moved on and the chunky rhino logo was now strongly associated with the SJ range. Owners were flashing their lights at each other on the road and a general four-wheel drive camaraderie was growing. It was at this time that Suzuki decided to organize an event for all these owners and that was how the first Rhino Rally, and ultimately the Suzuki Rhino Club, came about. As Ian Catford explains, it all started rather vaguely, built on the enthusiasm of the owners: "We didn't really know what we were going to do. We asked the All Wheel Drive Club to get involved, designing and marshalling an off-road course specifically for SJs. Well, it just grew from there. The first rally was at Castle Ashby and we had around 250-300 vehicles. There were a lot of very enthusiastic owners and it was a great day. That's when we knew we had started something."

It was from this first Rhino Rally that Suzuki produced a magazine to celebrate the event. From there the next obvious step was to organize a formal club – which is how the Suzuki Rhino Club was born. Membership is free to anyone buying a new or secondhand four-wheel drive Suzuki, and

The Rhino Rally was started with the enthusiasm of the SJ and Santana Suzuki owners and today has grown to be a major annual event.

entitles you to a very good colour magazine, *Rhino News*, plus free entry to the annual Rhino Rally. To date, the Rhino Club has some 25,000 members.

   The annual rally is an excellent place for you to try off-roading your Vitara for the first time. You may well arrive at the event with every intention of just parking your Vitara and having a look around, but when you see the fun fellow Suzuki owners are having, you're bound to join in pretty quickly.

There are usually sections where you can drive off-road according to your ability and experience, all ably marshalled by the guys from the All Wheel Drive Club. You will also find the likes of Chief Executive, John Norman, at the Rhino Rally, together with a large number of the 170 employees that work for Suzuki GB plc. It's that kind of event.

The 1993 Rhino Rally attracted over 4,000 people, including over 100 Dutch Suzuki four-wheel drive enthusiasts. Unfortunately, there was no rally

The Rhino rally is a great place to meet like-minded Vitara owners and it should certainly encourage you to take your vehicle off-road.

during 1994 because of the change of corporate details, Suzuki GB Cars ceasing to remain part of the Heron company and becoming Suzuki GB plc instead. Although the change has had no effect on the way the company is run, nor on the enthusiasm for running the Rhino Club, it did cause problems in preparing the 1994 Rally, so it was cancelled. At the time of writing, plans are well advanced for the 10th Rhino Rally in 1995.

On-going with the Rhino Club has been Suzuki's charity involvement to help protect *real* rhinos. Working with London Zoo and a vet, Robert Brett, Suzuki – and Suzuki owners and enthusiasts – have been supporting a project in Kenya aimed at saving the white rhino. By the end of 1994, Suzuki owners had contributed over £95,000 to the Save the Rhino charity. This is particularly impressive, and along with the Rhino Club makes for an interesting extension to Vitara ownership.

Suzuki 4x4 Driver Of The Year

A development from the Rhino Club in 1994 saw the introduction of the Suzuki 4x4 Driver of the Year competition. Run in conjunction with *Off Road & 4 Wheel Drive* magazine, the competition was open to all four-wheel drive enthusiasts, not just Suzuki owners. The initial part of the competition involved completing a written questionnaire. From this 12 finalists were chosen for a showdown in a testing environment in North Wales, on a site organized by the expert off-roading company, Motor Safari. The weather was freezing cold with lots of snow and ice to make the course particularly difficult. All entrants had to drive Vitaras, provided by Suzuki, even if some of them normally drove 'other' four-wheel drive vehicles. By the end of the

The Suzuki 4x4 Driver of the Year competition is organized in association with the monthly 4x4 magazine Off Road & 4 Wheel Drive. *The event puts competitors with a variety of experience over a difficult course, all driving similar specification Vitaras.*

competition, however, every competitor was very impressed by the way the Vitaras coped with the conditions.

The 1994 winner was John Mitchell, a storeman for an electrical company and owner of a Suzuki SJ, who won a superb trophy and a safari holiday in Kenya. It is expected that this will have been the start of an annual competition, and it is guaranteed that Vitaras will be used as the test vehicles. As you can see, there's a lot more to owning a Suzuki Vitara than you might first have imagined!

OFF ROAD
& 4 WHEEL DRIVE

The only accessory that your Vitara will ever need…

EVERY MONTH